Truth Stranger than Fiction

Truth Stranger than Fiction

Race, Realism and the U.S. Literary Marketplace

Augusta Rohrbach

palgrave

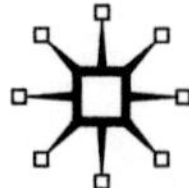

TRUTH STRANGER THAN FICTION: RACE, REALISM, AND THE U.S. LITERARY MARKETPLACE

First published 2002 by
PALGRAVE™
175 Fifth Avenue, New York, N.Y. 10010 and
Houndmills, Basingstoke, Hampshire, England RG21 6XS.
Companies and representatives throughout the world.

PALGRAVE is the new global publishing imprint of St. Martin's Press LLC Scholarly and Reference Division and Palgrave Publishers Ltd. (formerly Macmillan Press Ltd.).

ISBN 0–312–23921–1

Library of Congress Cataloging-in-Publication Data
Rohrbach, Augusta, 1961-
Truth stranger than fiction: race, realism, and the U.S. literary marketplace / Augusta Rohrbach.
p. cm.
Includes bibliographical references and index.
ISBN 0–312–23921–1
1. American fiction—19th century—History and criticism. 2. Race in literature. 3. Capitalism and literature—United States—History—19th century. 4. Economics and literature—United States—History—19th century. 5. Antislavery movements—United States—History—19th century. 6. Garrison, William Lloyd, 1805–1879—Influence. 7. African Americans in literature. 8. Realism in literature. 9. Slavery in literature. 10. Money in literature. I. Title.

PS374.R32 R64 2002
813'.30912—dc21

2001046162

A catalogue record for this book is available from the British Library.

Design by Letra Libre, Inc.
First edition: January 2002
10 9 8 7 6 5 4 3 2 1

Printed in the United States of America.

For my parents:

Herbert John Rohrbach, Jr.
Laura May Grayson
J. Gordon Grayson

Contents

List of Illustrations

Chapter I

Photographs by John Seigfried;
images used by permission of Mudd Library, Oberlin College.

Chapter 2

Photographs used by permission of
The Library Company of Philadelphia.

Chapter 3

Chapter 4

Photographs used by permission of
the Houghton Library, Harvard University

Acknowledgments

Research trips to the Schomburg Center for Research on Black Culture (1996), the Houghton Library (1997), the Mark Twain Papers at the Bancroft Library (1998), and the Library Company of Philadelphia (1999) have enabled me to study a wide range of material—from advertisements to unpublished photographs and letters—surrounding the development of realism and its cultural contexts. And support for those trips, from the Ford Foundation, Harvard University, the Library Company of Philadelphia, and Oberlin College, granted me access to these important resources. But collecting material is only part of the research process. And perhaps more important than the institutional generosity that has made this study possible is the personal and intellectual generosity of so many that I have come in contact with over the years.

First, Ann Douglas, who directed my dissertation, "Riddles of Identity: Ideologies of Race and Gender in Late-Nineteenth- and Early-Twentieth Century American Fiction," while I was a student at Columbia University, had an enormous impact on my thinking and research style. As her teaching assistant for many years, I learned to love the *story* of American literature. It was from Ann that I learned how to make a material argument and came to appreciate its full merit.

Of my fellow graduate students, I still remember important connections made in conversation and friendship with Cameron Broderick, Chris Castiglia, Alison Giffen, Jonathan Gross, Patrick Horrigan, Danell Jones, and J. Jordon Sullivan.

During my years at Oberlin, I had the very good fortune to know and work with Jan Cooper, Pat Day, Chris Howell, Wendy Kozol, Laurie McMillin, Scott McMillin, Whitney Pape, Paula Richman, David Walker, and Sandy Zagarell. I cherish the years spent, lessons learned, and softball played on balmy summer afternoons. And I still miss working with the members of my writing group—the cultural studies cult as we called ourselves. The fruitful exchange of work and ideas that circulated among us at our core when we were three—Paula Richman, Sandy Zagarell, and myself—animated this book in ways that were vital to its development and completion.

I left Oberlin under the most pleasant and productive of circumstances: to take up a Bunting Fellowship at the newly christened Radcliffe Institute for Advanced Study. During my time here—which was miraculously extended in collaboration with the W. E. B. DuBois Institute at Harvard University for a second year—I have been given extraordinary gifts: the joy of thinking, the pleasure of writing and the enormous privilege to have the time and the money to do both. Thanks to Rita Nakoshima Brock, Mary Dunn, and Henry Louis Gates, Jr., for making it possible and productive. My "sister fellows" Elizabeth Arnold, Anne Bailey, Suzy Becker, Denise Buell, Cathy Cohen, Lenore Cowen, Samantha Chang, Lisa Herschbach, Alice Jarrard, Francesca Polleta, Tina Rathbone, Francesca Sawaya, Vicki Schultz, Cathy Silber, Sylvia Spitta and Shellburne Thurber always had something worthwhile to say and made sure to take the trouble to say it. While I revised this manuscript on a Bunting Fellowship, I had the help of my Radcliffe Junior Research Partner, Avi Steinberg; he never stinted in his efforts to check both the logic and the facts of my writing. At Palgrave, Kristi Long, my editor, Donna Cherry, my production editor, and Annjeanette Kern and Aimee Hartmann, my copyeditors, made the publication process interesting and fun. Irene Goldman-Price, who kindly prepared the index, brought insight and clarity to the project in the last push to publication—one couldn't ask for more.

And, of course, countless others have helped this project along through their comments and questions. In addition to members of ASA, ALA, and MLA audiences, I am especially grateful to Huston Baker, Marcellous Blount, Larry Buell, Russ Castronovo, Joe Donahue, David Eng, Robert Fanuzzi, Henry Louis Gates, Jr., Steve Germic, Gordon Hutner, Robert Iltis, Margo Jefferson, Amy Kaplan, Kathryne Lindberg, the late Henry Mayer, Richard Newman, Laura Salz, Jack Salzman, and Carole Shaffer-Koros. Special mention goes to Lisa Herschbach. She urged me on in the last and difficult phases of completion, providing invaluable insight into the construction of the argument and the ways to streamline the book. The elegance of her mind is a thing of beauty to me. But it is Priscilla Wald who most deserves praise. She followed this work closely from its inception as a doctoral thesis at Columbia to its current incarnation. She believed in the book and knew to ask the right questions so I could believe in it too.

Throughout the last five years Larry Mayer kept the light on for me when all seemed dark and murky. Together we have survived to flourish in the ashen dander of our existence. And though along the way I have suffered some extreme losses, the death of my own father in 1984 and then my stepfather in 1997, I have always known that I am lucky even to have lost such greatness. Yes, indeed, I have been given many gifts, and I am grateful for each and every one.

Introduction

According to most literary histories of the United States, realism emerged after the Civil War and became a full-fledged genre by the 1880s. As a form, it is dominated by the novel and tends to describe the minutiae of everyday life within a social and economic context. Money usually figures largely as a central tension of the novel and in many cases the main characters in these novels have some problem—accentuated by finances. Lily Bart, Edith Wharton's famous heroine in *The House of Mirth,* for instance, is stuck without the social and financial support of marriage at age 29. Similarly, Isabel Archer in James's *Portrait of a Lady* is embroiled in the plots and counterplots that run through the novel by virtue of the money she is given. In other words, in all of these novels, money matters in important and life-changing ways. Thus, realists tend to be united thematically more so than they are stylistically.

What scholars have not done is follow the money, tracing its history to understand something about the source of money as a generic feature of realism. *Truth Stranger than Fiction: Race, Realism and the U.S. Literary Marketplace* explores legal tender as a narrative signifier peculiar to realism, but the approach the book takes is not solely literary. Rather, to discover the annals of capital within the context of American literature, I consult a series of nonliterary objects ranging from advertisements to photographs, contracts, and checkbooks. Through an examination of this archive, I map the role that money played in the formation of realism by using the lens of business history to reread this literary history. Thus, this book resituates realism, locating its origins 50 years earlier than usual in Garrisonian abolition—a movement that gave rise to all manner of material production, from "free-labor" shoes to slave narratives, sermons, and fictional works.

If we resituate the origins of realism in abolitionist activity, then William Lloyd Garrison emerges as a major catalyst for the growth of literary realism in the United States. But how can Garrison—who died in 1879—be related to a literary movement that had not yet been born? And why connect a radical abolitionist who devoted his life to his campaign for the immediate emancipation of slaves in the United States to what many see as a moribund literary style devoted to the depiction of middle-class white people?

Few realize that most of the people who had a hand in the development of realism in the United States wore two hats—one for abolition and the other for realism. What are the factors that seem most relevant to this unlikely pairing? Abolition and the early glimmerings of realism both shared the same historical context. First, the combustible relationship between morality and money in nineteenth-century America played a central role: the religiosity of the period and the developing ethos of liberal capitalism came together in the abolitionist movement. Simultaneously, the rise of print culture—a product of technology and the industrial revolution—offered a means to profit from a growing interest in the abolition of slavery as well as other reform movements.[1] Advertisements in *The Liberator,* for example, make clear that the products for sale address social and political issues at the very heart of nineteenth-century New England culture—issues that came to define the meaning of citizenship within American culture at large. Capital, for Garrisonians and their ilk, can and should be used to support and develop the reform spirit at the center of the movement. Thus, money flowed most freely when reform was at stake, explaining, in part, the enormous popularity of slave narratives in the nineteenth-century literary marketplace.

Positioning literature squarely within this marketplace, I trace the influence of generic conventions popularized in slave narratives—such as the use of authenticating details, money as a signifier of personal suffering, as well as the use of dialect and a frank treatment of the body—for later realist writings. I see these generic borrowings as part of the effort white writers made to harness a style that effectively mobilized readers toward social action. Remarkably, this aspect of literary history has been, as Toni Morrison would say, "covered up" by the political exigencies of the marketplace and of literary history itself.[2] African Americans (and not necessarily or always solely African American writing) had a determining influence on canonical realism. Through the fight to abolish slavery in the United States, they forced a set of conventions (initiating a reformist edge on [sentimental] verisimilitude) tied intimately to economic imperatives.[3]

Considering abolition as a central context for literary realism helps us understand the bond that unites an otherwise disparate group of writers. United by an ethos rather than a literary aesthetic, realist texts hold much in common with abolitionist writings. For instance, in evaluating American antislavery publications in 1838, abolitionist James Birney asserted that these writings "cannot be classed according to any particular style of quality of composition. They may be characterized generally, as well suited to affect the public mind—to rouse into healthful activity the conscience of this nation, stupefied, torpid, almost dead, in relation to Human Rights, the high theme of which they treat."[4] The same may be said of later realist texts. They do not have, as one of realism's most recent critics, Michael Davitt Bell, has observed, "a specific kind of literary representation" guided by a doctrine of artistic standards.[5] Rather, realism holds to a set of social values. Its practitioners—no matter how distinct in other ways—share the belief that literature has a social purpose. They view the pen as, perhaps, not mightier than the sword, but certainly as a powerful instrument capable of transforming the hearts and minds of readers.

I call this realism "humanitarian realism" because it is closely linked with the reform movements fueled by the liberal capitalism of the mid-nineteenth century. In dubbing realism "humanitarian realism," I am drawing on Thomas W. Laqueur's reading of the relationship between the depiction of human suffering and the moral imperative to put a stop to such suffering. As I will discuss in the following pages, realism has its roots in what Laqueur has called the "humanitarian narrative"—one that uses the physical details of the body and its suffering to engender moral action in readers.[6] In the history of American literature, realism stands out as a genre with a profoundly social conscience.

Rather than evaluate realism's success (or failure) at prompting social change as previous critics have done, I am more interested in understanding how and why realist writers came to believe that literature holds the power to elicit social justice.[7] Connecting the development of realism with the abolitionist movement opens up the way for understanding realism's roots in an American context of social struggle.[8] All of the writers featured in this study—Frederick Douglass, Sojourner Truth, Rose Terry Cooke, William Dean Howells, and Edith Wharton—sought to harness the energies of the marketplace and thus propel their own careers *through* the causes they embraced.

This book considers race, genre, and marketplace as constitutive of the matrix of late-nineteenth- and early-twentieth-century culture in the United States. Each chapter focuses on specific cultural institutions, central personages, and historic turning points as contexts for the formation of the literary genre of realism in American literature. One by one, the chapters pose and explore a set of questions about the shifting relationship between literature and culture in the United States from 1830 on by focusing on evolving trends in literary realism.

The question at the heart of chapter 1, How does Garrisonian abolition shape a context for realism?, leads me to an examination of advertisements for slave narratives and other literary productions. Taking stock of these narratives' staggering popularity, the second chapter asks: How do slave narratives—heralded as the first "indigenous" literature by Theodore

Parker—affect the developing profession of authorship? In the third chapter, I use the work and career of Rose Terry Cooke to explore scholarship's failure to see the relationship between the literary features of the slave narratives and the development of regional literature, realism's precursor. As the book presses on toward the early twentieth century, I consider the ways that William Dean Howells's writings embody the cultural tensions of publishing as the business sought to profit from the development of American literary culture.

The last chapter builds on questions that align aesthetic and financial issues with the buried relevance of race as a factor in the literary marketplace. In "The Manner of the Marketplace: Edith Wharton as a Race Writer," I examine how Wharton adapts realism's conventions to lead to her own novelistic success. Railing against realism's penchant for lower-class characters and circumstances, Wharton alters the genre by treating race as class. Wharton's transformation of realism's humanitarian focus on social justice for blacks and later the lower classes to a concern for whites and the upper classes was a means to connect with a growing middle-class readership. The *House of Mirth* was the first of three bestselling novels she would write.[9]

In the epilogue to *Truth Stranger than Fiction: Race, Realism and the U.S. Literary Marketplace,* I explore how realism continues to inform our own literary tastes. The popularity of memoir as a genre signals a return of favor for "fact" over "fiction" in our own time. Many modern-day memoirists such as Frank McCourt and Mary Karr dwell on the disadvantages of class rather than racial inequalities as a way to capture audience interest and empathy: their version of humanitarian realism. These are twentieth-century efforts to "keep it real" learned from nineteenth-century publishing history—the history beneath American realism.

By naming this last section "Keeping it Real," I am calling attention to the link between African American culture and the literary history of the United States. "Keeping it real" is an expression taken from black English that permeates today's hip-hop culture. When a person "keeps it real," his or her actions represent a degree of authenticity—or realness—a palpable link to the ordinary everyday world. The authors under consideration here "keep it real" through their skillful play with three features: race as an organizing principle of American culture, genre as a formal means for expression, and the market as the place where it all comes together.

“Truth Stranger and Stronger than Fiction”

Reexamining William Lloyd Garrison’s *The Liberator*[1]

In the words of James Russell Lowell, poet and fellow abolitionist, William Lloyd Garrison “knew how types were set,/ He had a dauntless spirit and a press.”[2] What people have yet to appreciate fully are the larger purposes that Garrisonian abolition has served in the development of American literary culture. Propelled by his own dictum to be “as harsh as truth,” Garrison published many slave narratives, including Frederick Douglass’s famous 1845 narrative.[3] An increase in attention to literature’s moral purpose and an emerging taste for the “real” share the same ground in *The Liberator.* Through a range of publishing practices—from the publication of advertisements to that of slave narratives—Garrison’s newspaper helped to crystallize the taste for the “real” and was thus formative in the development of the literary genre we call realism.

The longest running abolitionist newspaper, William Lloyd Garrison’s *The Liberator* (1831–65) was a product of a nineteenth-century marketplace—concerned with morality, money, and veracity. The print emissary of Garrisonian abolition, this newspaper epitomized “the vanguard of capitalist liberalism.”[4] By virtue of their connection to the abolitionist cause, objects of everyday use—from candy to shoes—were sold in the pages of *The Liberator.* The affiliation between material culture and a moral agenda also carried over to the literary marketplace: a book’s relationship to abolitionist agendas was frequently used to sell it in the pages of *The Liberator.* The moral basis for commercial practices, epitomized in Garrisonian abolition, became a product's main selling point in Garrison's paper. Thus, every section of *The Liberator* called for active moral participation in the cause of abolition through social, political, and commercial practices.[5] *The Liberator*'s dual relationship with liberal capitalism and moral suasion makes it an ideal vehicle for the study of realism, a literary style that is closely linked with money and morality.

I. "I Will Be as Harsh as Truth": Garrison's Appeal to Readers

Abolitionist culture—fostered by antislavery societies and their publications—gave rise to all manner of cultural production that, in turn, yielded a new and lively marketplace for ideas, goods, and services related to the cause. William Lloyd Garrison (1805–1879) and *The Liberator* are two important products of the age, created out of the historical tension that was at the center of abolition: the need to make a living in a capitalist world without violating the evangelical morality of the mid-nineteenth century.[6]

Garrison used the cause of abolition as a unique way to make a living while furthering his moral principles. Unlike gentleman reformers such as Wendell Phillips, Garrison had grown up knowing that he would have to support himself and his family. His father, a seaman with a taste for rum, deserted the family when Garrison was just three years old. His mother, a strong-willed Baptist, struggled to keep the family together. Garrison started contributing to the household at age five by selling homemade molasses candy on the street corners of Newburyport, Massachusetts.[7]

Garrison had shown a savvy market-conscious nature, starting from his first pseudonymous writings in the *Newburyport Herald* at the beginning of his career in 1818, and had always known that the way to succeed would be to learn to sell himself in the marketplace of ideas. According to James Brewer Stewart, one of Garrison's biographers, Garrison was driven at an early age by the Franklinian ideal of the self-made man who measured his success in terms of his ability to create and adjust to market conditions.[8] But Garrison's efforts to build a career took shape in a uniquely nineteenth-century way. His personal need to make a living was intimately linked with his contemporary culture's need to do so by morally informed means.[9] Throughout his career, Garrison never lost sight of the necessity to balance his welfare with that of the cause, and therefore, never allowed money concerns to eclipse his moral ones. In order for Garrison to be successful, abolition must be too.[10]

Perhaps it was the combination of Garrison's sheer scrappiness and his moral commitment that attracted his benefactors. In order to promote the cause, Garrison founded *The Liberator* in 1831. As editor of the only abolitionist paper to survive 34 years of continuous publication, Garrison created and held a market that impressed and attracted supporters. Even once the abolition movement had splintered into several factions, *The Liberator* remained, despite its idiosyncrasies, the publication that people most closely associated with the cause.[11]

Of course, the racism that was a significant part of the abolitionist movement played an important role in *The Liberator*'s success. Black abolitionist newspapers suffered for their radicalness by dying of economic failure.[12] Not so for *The Liberator;* this paper used the black cause for its appeal and capitalized on its radicalness. Run by a white man, the paper tapped revenues not readily available to black abolitionist newspapers. For one thing, the paper geared itself toward a white readership while it also enjoyed the support and attention of blacks. As a result of its appeal to readers on both sides of the color line, the paper offered access to a wider range of the population and thus could attract advertisers interested in expanding the marketplace beyond the racial limits that held sway during the period.

Its beginnings, however, did not augur well for its success. Early on in its development, the white New York businessmen Arthur and Lewis Tappan, among others, funded the paper. But aside from the bevy of free blacks in Philadelphia who supported the paper, Garrison's subscriber base remained scant. Working outside of and against the "press-gang system," Garrison eschewed the subsidized favor of societies and political organizations.[13] Rather than jeopardize his autonomy as an editor by accepting funds that might have strings attached, Garrison cultivated the sale of advertising to cover operating expenses.

Such revenues were not available to black abolitionist papers whose relatively short life spans provide further evidence of their precarious place in a market dominated by whites. A review of the advertisements that appeared in these papers confirms their limited circulation. Of the sample considered here, *The Colored American* alone had an advertising section featuring print media. All others had ads for local goods and services only. Advertisements for books made up a significant portion of all the ads that appear. Yet, though books are advertised, novels are not. An 1839 article might explain this exclusion; it concludes that "most novels and romances have no value because they are immoral."[14] Here, too, we see the effects of racism on the reading habits of African Americans. These readers cannot afford to be titillated by "stories" of slavery as can the whites who read *The Liberator.* Readers of *The Colored American* shunned fiction, perhaps for its long association with lying. The clever lies that helped many out of slavery were put aside for the moral high ground made available by freedom.[15] Slavery was (and *is*) a horrifying reality, not the stuff of sensationalistic fiction.

The racial composition of Garrison's readership offered advertisers a wide audience of potential customers whose interests provided them with a known basis on which to hawk their wares.[16] This audience might more properly be called readers rather than subscribers, because *The Liberator* circulated throughout the country largely by means of "exchanges"—a systematic distribution to over one hundred periodicals.[17] These exchanges worked as an ingenious way to gain notoriety, which, in turn, increased *The Liberator*'s visibility.

Garrison would send his paper to Southern editors, who, enraged by the views it held, would reprint sections as proof of the Yankee abolitionist threat. Readers would respond and then Northern papers would reprint Southern responses for their sensationalist value. Of course, Garrison would reprint all of it.[18] Thus *The Liberator*'s sphere of influence far exceeded the few white philanthropists and small communities of free people of color from New York and Philadelphia that made up its subscriber list. Garrison, like his contemporary P. T. Barnum, who used the method of anonymous letters to attract attention to his "exhibits," saw the tools of the impresario as a means to spread his message and gain an audience.[19]

Advertising, in its many forms, would be a key tool for financing *The Liberator* and maintaining Garrison's autonomy as its editor. He knew that if he relinquished control of *The Liberator* he would also lose control of his career. For instance, he resisted offers to make the paper solvent by converting it into the organ of the American Antislavery Society (AAS) more than once. Keeping the paper a free agent for the cause meant keeping the market for reform open. Unwilling to give up on his ideals—his beliefs in the perfectibility of humankind, and the belief that slavery should be abolished completely and immediately rather than gradually (the second being the most repugnant to the higher-ups in the AAS) Garrison refused to give up what we would currently call his market share.[20] It is precisely *The Liberator*'s hold on the market, earned by radical views supported by an innovative style and font in printing, that brought advertisers to the paper. Only in making his views known by first making them noticeable could Garrison and *The Liberator* succeed.

Garrison's address to his public in *The Liberator*'s inaugural issue might help us understand his editorial vision concerning its role in the cause for abolition. In this initial editorial, Garrison insists that he "will be as harsh as truth, and as uncompromising as justice." He concludes his explosive address by asserting his intention to use the paper and his voice in it to abolish slavery. "I am in earnest—I will not equivocate—I will not excuse—I will not retreat a single inch—**AND I WILL BE HEARD** . . ." he exploded.[21] Here, Garrison—profoundly influenced by his own immediatism—establishes an important link between language and action. He equates the rigor of his message with its meaning; form follows content in *The Liberator.*

The text badgers on a visual level as well. One of the first things that would strike the nineteenth-century reader of this declaration is the use of italics and capital letters. As Garrison "reached for the upper case" to make his statement emphatically, he abandoned the traditional standard agate 5 1/2 point type—used for advertising and news stories alike—as the first phase of his attack on the reader's sensible, uniform world.[22] And Garrison's message is no less destructive of the status quo. Garrison's willingness to be an iconoclast lent itself well to his cause. He pressed the cause through articles, lectures, pamphlets, handbills, and posters—all basic methods that P. T. Barnum grouped under the heading of advertising.[23] Garrison's efforts were carefully calculated according to the principles of advertising emerging at this time. The articles he reprinted, the letters he published, and the advertisements that appeared were all orchestrated to engender moral action in accordance with his views on abolition and related topics. The paper gave expression to what Thomas Laqueur has called the "humanitarian narrative": through its various features, *The Liberator* appealed to supporters of abolition and thus established itself as abolition's representative voice.[24]

II. Typography Unbound: Advertising in *The Liberator*

"I have delighted in nothing more as regards to manual work, than the manipulation of types," Garrison averred a year before his death.[25] Throughout his long career, Garrison showed his love of the art of printing in his willingness to set ads varying in all manner of presentation, thus attracting advertisers and a reading public.[26] In this area, as in his use of invective, Garrison led the way toward equating the ability to get attention with the ability to succeed. In effect, Garrison was teaching advertisers that getting consumer attention was tantamount to a sale. *The Liberator*'s de facto circulation, combined with his willingness to experiment typographically, attracted advertisers, and kept them advertising in its pages.

Newspapers have always had a symbiotic relationship with advertising. In fact, advertisements were originally treated as news items, or "notices."[27] Well into the 1850s, they could be found on the first page of newspapers and were also interspersed with news stories.[28] In keeping with the trend to use advertisements to develop reader interest, publishers insisted on fresh advertising copy. Newspaper editors forced advertisers to rewrite ads for each issue—rather than rerun old advertising copy—because they knew ads were part of what sold papers. Information about recently available

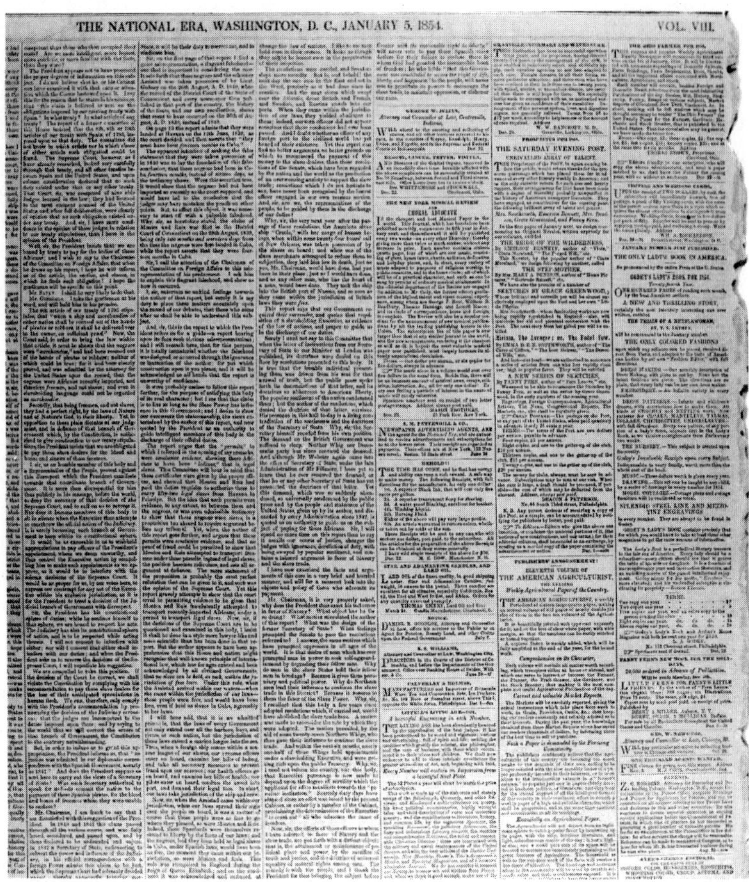

THE NATIONAL ERA, WASHINGTON, D. C., JANUARY 5, 1854. VOL. VIII.

Figure 1.1: Advertising page from *The National Era,* 5 January 1854. Photograph by John Seigfried; image used by permission of Mudd Library, Oberlin College.

products, supplies, and inventions was considered important news. By the late 1850s, however, advertisements were no longer welcomed bits of information; they promoted products competitive with one another and were therefore considered intrusions on the reader's sensibility. Readers of *Gleason's Pictorial* (1851–54; later *Ballou's Pictorial,* 1855–59) for instance, so objected to the intrusion of advertisements in an 1855 issue that ads were eliminated from future issues altogether.[29] Many periodicals tried to generate adequate revenue from subscriptions, but most had to turn to advertisers to sustain themselves.

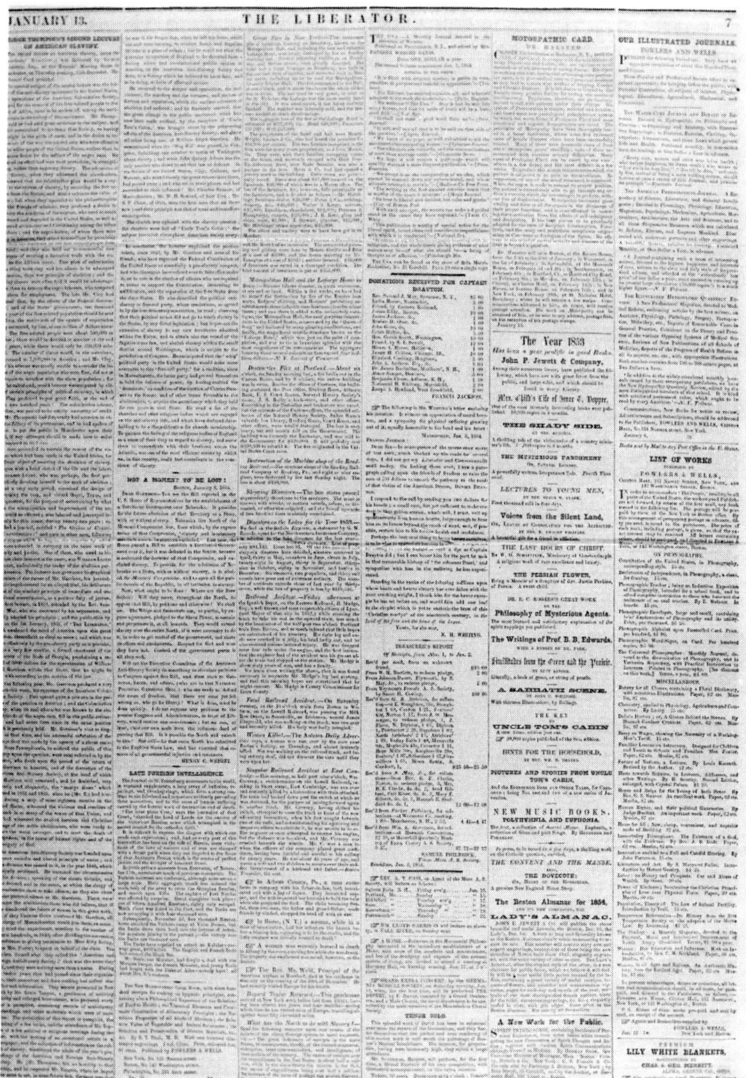
JANUARY 13. THE LIBERATOR. 7

DONATIONS RECEIVED FOR CAPTAIN DRAYTON.

The Year 1853

John P. Jewett & Company.

THE SHADY SIDE.

Voices from the Silent Land.

THE PERSIAN FLOWER.

The Writings of Prof. B. B. Edwards.

A SABBATH SCENE.

UNCLE TOM'S CABIN

NEW MUSIC BOOKS.

The Boston Almanac for 1854.

LADY'S ALMANAC.

A New Work for the Public.

OUR ILLUSTRATED JOURNALS.

LIST OF WORKS

LILY WHITE BLANKETS.

Figure 1.2 Advertising page from *The Liberator,* 13 January 1854. Photograph by John Seigfried; image used by permission of Mudd Library, Oberlin College.

The reluctance of newspapers to give advertisers free reign is registered in the one control that editors and publishers were able to exercise on advertisers: standardization. All ads were printed in agate print, and were limited to three inches and one column.

As you can see from the reproduction of the advertising section of *The National Era,* little effort is made toward distinguishing one advertisement from the next (see figure 1.1). Often abdicating responsibility for advertisers' claims, many papers wished to dissociate themselves from the products they advertised. The editor of *The National Era,* Gamaliel Baily, for instance, disavowed any responsibility for the products advertised there. Editors frequently did not allow varying display type so as to simplify printing procedures and also so that no advertiser had the advantage over any other—a way of democratizing capitalism that earlier entrepreneurs such as P. T. Barnum had already begun to challenge.[30]

Garrison broke with this practice. He not only chose his advertisers according to their views on abolition, it was common knowledge that he gave free advertising space to the patent medicines that he found helpful. A quick glance at the advertising page of approximately the same date of publication as that of *The National Era* (reproduced in figure 1.1), will show the degree to which Garrison promoted a competitive market through the use of typeface, size, woodcuts and layout design. (See figure 1.2.)
Though also grouped together as in *The National Era,* these advertisements make use of blank space and varied typeface to attract the reader. *The Liberator*'s masthead demonstrates how important advertising was to the paper. Beginning in 1839, rates for advertising became a stable part of the masthead, just as they were in later successful dailies such at the *New York Times*—further evidence of Garrison's desire to make the cause a commercial venture. (See figure 1.3.)

The freedom given to advertisers in *The Liberator* to use moral and political outrage toward slavery as a means to attract attention and sell products

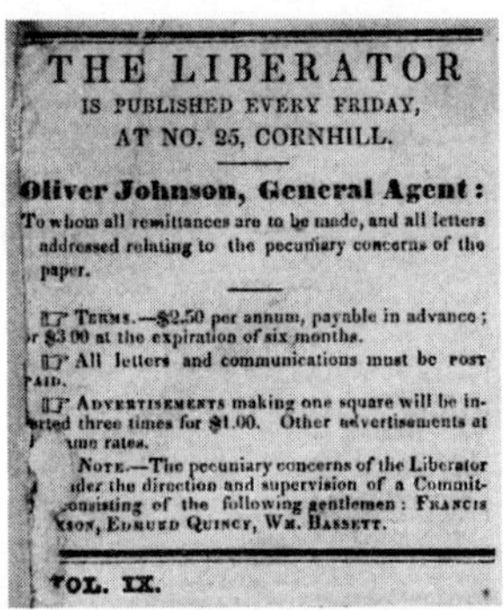

THE LIBERATOR
IS PUBLISHED EVERY FRIDAY,
AT NO. 25, CORNHILL.

Oliver Johnson, General Agent:
To whom all remittances are to be made, and all letters addressed relating to the pecuniary concerns of the paper.

☞ TERMS.—$2.50 per annum, payable in advance; or $3.00 at the expiration of six months.

☞ All letters and communications must be POST PAID.

☞ ADVERTISEMENTS making one square will be inserted three times for $1.00. Other advertisements at ame rates.

NOTE.—The pecuniary concerns of the Liberator der the direction and supervision of a Committ- onsisting of the following gentlemen: FRANCIS KSON, EDMUND QUINCY, WM. BASSETT.

VOL. IX.

Figure 1.3 The left side of *The Liberator*'s masthead, 4 January 1839. Photograph by John Seigfried; image used by permission of Mudd Library, Oberlin College.

must have encouraged prospective advertisers to do the same. Books, magazines, dry goods, clothing and even resorts were developed in response to the mounting fervor of abolition. By making advertising such a recognizable aspect of *The Liberator,* Garrison provided space for advertisers to cultivate the taste for the political power in the consumer.[31] Just as Victorianism spread through the United States in part through the taste for victoriana, so, too, did abolitionist ideology began to make itself felt in market terms.[32]

The Liberator identified an emerging market of people who would put their money where their morals were by buying nonslave-produced, "free-labor" goods and services. This market is akin to our own emerging "cruelty-free" products; such products supply animal rights supporters with the items they enjoy while reducing the moral conflicts in the purchase. Inspired by an earlier movement of antislavery Quakers, such as the Hicks and Motts in the 1830s, abolitionists supported a boycott of the products of slavery. And the call for the "entire abstinence from the products of slavery" created the market for free-labor products.[33] Advertisements for free-labor sugar—"a beautiful article"—promised to satisfy the customer's sweet tooth as well as a taste for what we currently call the politically correct. (See figure 1.4.)

These early ads assume a singular symmetry between their message and the consumer. Persuasive language is absent—the assumption here is that the products aren't being *sold* to the consumer so much as they are simply being *provided* for the customer. They belong, historically speaking, to an earlier epoch of advertising—one in which ads are sources of information rather than tools of persuasion.[34] The candy wrappers of "free sweets" were decorated with an early version of the advertising jingle. Antislavery couplets rewarded and affirmed the customer's choice to purchase free-labor goods. One such couplet rhymed out its warning that "If slavery comes by color, which God gave,/ Fashion may change, and you become the slave."[35] The blurb for free-labor shoes and boots running in a January 1839 issue of *The Liberator* assured its readers that the manufacturer "intends to entirely avoid the use of materials produced by unrequited labor of the slave"(see figure 1:4). This ad promises a product that offers a kind of moral and spiritual salvation rather than a material one.

This ad for free-labor shoes and boots taps into the vital connection between abolition and the growing forces of the woman's movement, another development of an American cultural consciousness that had its roots in abolitionist activity.[36] The ads that appear in *The Liberator* take for granted the notion that women are powerful consumers—many of the products are for female consumption only.[37] And these ads work on the assumption that consumers' self-images are linked to what they purchase: buying "free labor" makes them members of a society that does not rely on slave labor for its comforts or necessities. In this light, these ads provide

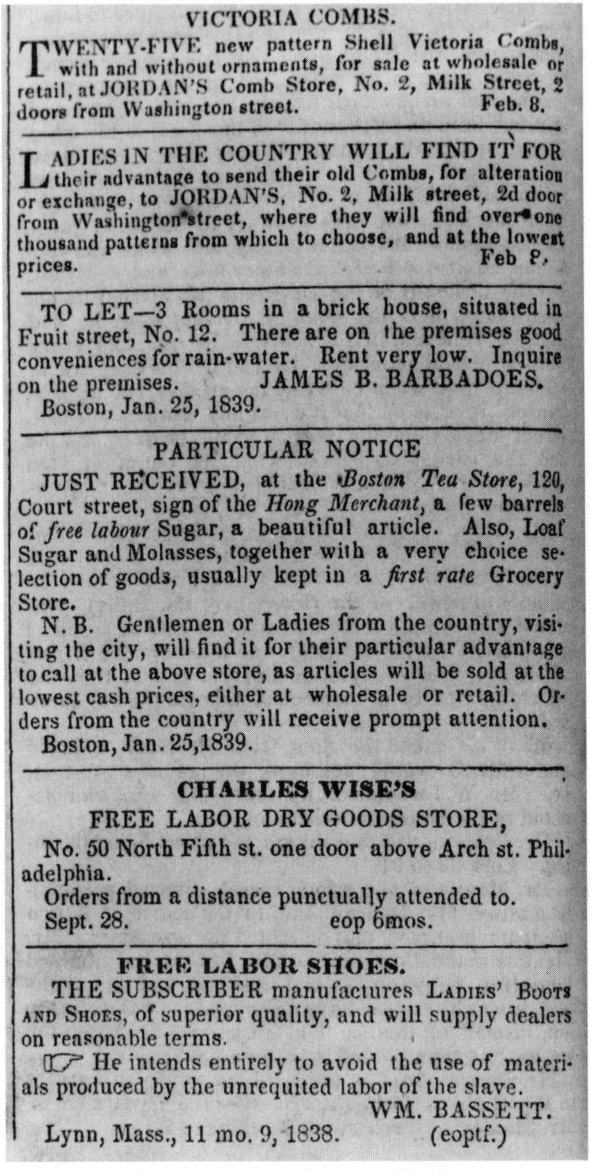

VICTORIA COMBS.

TWENTY-FIVE new pattern Shell Victoria Combs, with and without ornaments, for sale at wholesale or retail, at JORDAN'S Comb Store, No. 2, Milk Street, 2 doors from Washington street. Feb. 8.

LADIES IN THE COUNTRY WILL FIND IT FOR their advantage to send their old Combs, for alteration or exchange, to JORDAN'S, No. 2, Milk street, 2d door from Washington street, where they will find over one thousand patterns from which to choose, and at the lowest prices. Feb 8.

TO LET—3 Rooms in a brick house, situated in Fruit street, No. 12. There are on the premises good conveniences for rain-water. Rent very low. Inquire on the premises. JAMES B. BARBADOES.

Boston, Jan. 25, 1839.

PARTICULAR NOTICE

JUST RECEIVED, at the *Boston Tea Store*, 120, Court street, sign of the *Hong Merchant*, a few barrels of *free labour* Sugar, a beautiful article. Also, Loaf Sugar and Molasses, together with a very choice selection of goods, usually kept in a *first rate* Grocery Store.

N. B. Gentlemen or Ladies from the country, visiting the city, will find it for their particular advantage to call at the above store, as articles will be sold at the lowest cash prices, either at wholesale or retail. Orders from the country will receive prompt attention.

Boston, Jan. 25,1839.

CHARLES WISE'S

FREE LABOR DRY GOODS STORE,

No. 50 North Fifth st. one door above Arch st. Philadelphia.

Orders from a distance punctually attended to.

Sept. 28. eop 6mos.

FREE LABOR SHOES.

THE SUBSCRIBER manufactures LADIES' BOOTS AND SHOES, of superior quality, and will supply dealers on reasonable terms.

☞ He intends entirely to avoid the use of materials produced by the unrequited labor of the slave.

WM. BASSETT.

Lynn, Mass., 11 mo. 9, 1838. (eoptf.)

Figure 1.4 Advertisement from *The Liberator,* 1 March 1839. Photograph by John Seigfried; image used by permission of Mudd Library, Oberlin College.

a glimpse into the construction of a specifically American market because they sell products developed in response to and defined by the American context of slavery.

The abolitionist market included confections—such as sugar and molasses—imported from the Sandwich Islands, rather than transported from the slave South. Yet the needs that such free-labor trade could meet extended beyond the luxuries of sugar and molasses: Free-labor products were available to satisfy even the most everyday needs and budgets. In a dry goods store in Philadelphia, for example, all dry goods and sundries were produced by free-labor sources (see last advertisement in figure 1.4). And as a convenience to its customers, the store offered to send "orders from a distance punctually." This service signals the presence of an expanding market made possible by railroad and transportation improvements that reduced the significance of distance as an obstacle to trade.

Recognizing that *The Liberator*'s readership extended as far as Missouri and Kansas, the advertisements for free-labor products are a testament in market terms to a growing consciousness on a national, rather than a regional, scale much in the same way that the establishment of the Republican party in 1854 is in political terms. Many of these advertisers saw the potential for a nationalizing consciousness promoted by antislavery sentiment as an expanding marketplace. They placed advertisements in abolitionist newspapers such as *The Liberator* assuming a market beyond the paper's immediate circulation in Boston.

Part of the free-labor product's appeal to us as literary historians and students of American culture is that they grant us insight into a marketplace very different from our modern consumer culture. Not yet the era of what William Dean Howells would call "gimcrackeries," the mid-nineteenth-century market adapted to the preexisting desires of the customer, rather than creating those needs so as to satisfy them. As Ann Fabian observes, published slave narratives "helped members of an extended movement to imagine themselves as a community of like-minded workers."[38] With these products, there comes an appeal to consumption as a way to unite people and create community.[39] Such ads at once create and attest to a growing market along the lines of Benedict Anderson's concept of "imagined communities"; they use a shared ideological system to unite an otherwise disparate community whose members, as Anderson notes, "will never know most of their fellow members, meet them, or even hear of them, yet in the minds of each lives the image of their communion."[40]

Yet readers of *The Liberator* also offer us a model that differs significantly from Anderson's concept. Readers make themselves creators of and actors in the reform movement through their participation. Reading practices, letter writing, and purchases are all featured activities promoted through the composition of *The Liberator;* from columns, printed letters and advertisements, reader and newspaper interact and mutually constitute each other.[41] Reading the advertisements, for instance, one senses that customers are not being seduced into a sale as much as being encourages to exercise their "right" to buy, thus recognizing the link between politics and capital.[42] To modern eyes, free-labor products might resemble what we call promotional "tie-in" products. Purchase of such products created a sense of unified thought and action thus allowing the public to identify and participate through consumption. However, products advertised in *The Liberator* are less like "tie-in" products designed to give the public a vicarious experience of identification and participation though consumption. Rather, the products advertised in *The Liberator* are calls to action.

Businesses advertising in *The Liberator* or *The National Era* knew that in order to survive, they had to appeal to a culture fastidious about its commitment to reform. Free-labor products and the advertisements designed to sell them show that those who purchased these products, read these books and turned the pages of these newspapers were conscientiously doing so as a way of expressing their commitment to the abolition of slavery. This dimension of the abolitionist community is critical to our understanding of the marketplace as being fundamentally participatory and reflective of "real" social engagement. Abolition—like slavery—is a *lived* concept.

III. The Liberator's Liberties

Garrison took advantage of what seemed like an ever-expanding market niche by making use of other forms of narrative in the pages of *The Liberator.* He made a common practice, for instance, of publishing letters of regret from famous abolitionists who were "unable" to attend events that Garrison was supporting. He also printed letters censuring businesses, other periodicals, and towns and villages for practices he condemned. A tar-and-feathering episode in Kansas or reports of ill-treatment received in South Carolina as well as a letter exposing a female fugitive slave imposter all appeared in the pages of *The Liberator.* [43]

A "soft" form of advertising made popular by P. T. Barnum, the published letter to the editor, was a mainstay for the *Liberator* reader—"the REAL voice of REAL readers."[44] Garrison printed a wide range of letters in the weekly column, using the connection to real life as a way to build the cause and solidify the relationship among readers. Some of the letters he selected for publication dealt with issues directly related to slavery—reactions to the Kansas-Nebraska Act or the Fugitive Slave Act—but most dealt with the culture that was growing up around abolition as a social phenomenon. These letters concern the daily lives of readers, and thus reflect a commitment to the ordinary nature of human experience and to the large movement toward realism. Those chosen by Garrison for publication reflect his penchant for realism. Many letters adopted a tone "as harsh as truth," never shrinking from topics that might otherwise have not been published, a further link to literary realism's taste for the mundane and unseemly.

Garrison exploited the quotidian focus of readers' letters and through them united readers in "moments of identification" with each other because of their beliefs in a common cause.[45] For instance, Garrison published a letter from Anna Douglass, wife of the fugitive slave and prominent abolitionist, Frederick Douglass. Ignoring the fact that she remained illiterate all her life, Garrison chose to print this letter in which she wished to inform Garrison and his readers that "a certain person in the office" is not "causing unhappiness" in her house.[46] In this case, the letter-to-the-editor is used to quell a rumor of domestic discord, and Garrison's publication of it indicates how closely knit he wanted the movement to appear despite various kinds of internal strife. A letter such as this one might be used to show Douglass in an ordinary and "real" light. Douglass, an internationally known public speaker, is liable to suffer from rumors of domestic discord; despite his fame, he's just like anybody else. The letter also shows us that *The Liberator* readers considered the quotidian details of abolition and its figures an important part of their expressed interest.

Garrison furthered the keen sense of community among the readers of *The Liberator* by printing what may be the earliest known "personal" ad. A self-identified nineteen-year-old woman wrote to inform "marriageable males of her desirability and availability" in a letter published in January 1856.[47] Readers of *The Liberator* were encouraged to read abolition, write abolition, think abolition, eat abolition, and even marry abolition. This letter joins others on related subjects such as Quaker courting practices and the merits of new women's fashions.[48]

In other cases, letters to the editor were used to establish, promote, or censure business ventures through evidence of ordinary people's experiences. Take, for instance, a letter written by W. S. George, extolling the virtues of diet reform; in it he recommends hydropathic and vegetarian diets especially.[49] This letter, and so many others like it, are part of a trend in *The Liberator* to use the letter format as a form of personal endorsement and thus as an advertising tool. The attentive reader will often find the letter's commercial counterpart in the advertising section of the paper.

Such letters, including one written by William Wells Brown to announce the publication of his novel *Clotel,* help to promote sales. The prominent presence of the letter to the editor as a reliable source of public opinion also improves the credibility of the publication. The letter of endorsement calls attention to the symbiotic relationship between Garrison's readers and advertisers. All are engaged—by different means—in the struggle for the same end: the abolition of slavery.

The evolution of this relationship can be observed through sampling of ads run by one of *The Liberator*'s longest standing advertisers, a Boston clothing store owned by the black abolitionist, Lewis Hayden. An anonymous letter of endorsement, heralding the success of Lewis Hayden's clothing store appeared in the letter-to-the-editor section of *The Liberator* in January 1853 (see figure 1.5). The advertising section of the same issue also featured the ad that appears below:

LEWIS HAYDEN,

FASHIONABLE CLOTHING STORE,

No. 107 Cambridge Street.

Figure 1.5 Advertisement from *The Liberator,* 6 June 1851. Photographed by John Seigfried; image used by permission of Mudd Library, Oberlin College.

CLOTHING!

NEW STORE,

No. 107, : : : CAMBRIDGE STREET.

LEWIS HAYDEN

HAS opened the above Store, and keeps a good assortment of

MEN'S AND BOY'S CLOTHING,

of superior quality. Formerly a slave in Kentucky, he trusts that all will lend him a helping hand; as it will be his constant endeavor to keep for sale a good and cheap article on hand, both at wholesale and retail. tf April 4

Figure 1.6 Advertisement from *The Liberator,* 20 June 1851. Photographed by John Seigfried; image used by permission of Mudd Library, Oberlin College.

Following basic advertising conventions, Hayden's ad is hardly distinguished from the others that surround it. In the very next issue, however, the type and copy have been substantially changed. (See figure 1.6) Clearly, whoever wrote the copy for this ad—and more than likely it was Garrison himself—saw slavery's value as a selling tool as well. Part of the attention-getting visuals of the ad are the use of all caps, bold face, italics, and layout design. But the narrative importance of the fact that Hayden was formerly a slave in Kentucky is given prominence over cost and quality of the goods for sale. The mention of his slave status is also striking because Hayden would be well known not only to those in the Boston area but to abolitionists generally as a key operator of the underground railroad. His was the house, for instance, in which William Craft—author of the very popular slave narrative, *One Hundred Miles to Freedom*—hid while his wife Ellen posed as a white woman elsewhere. It was also in Hayden's house that the Crafts were formally married by the Reverend Theodore Parker.

A little later in 1853, however, Hayden's status as a former slave had become just one of many market lures in the advertisements for his store:

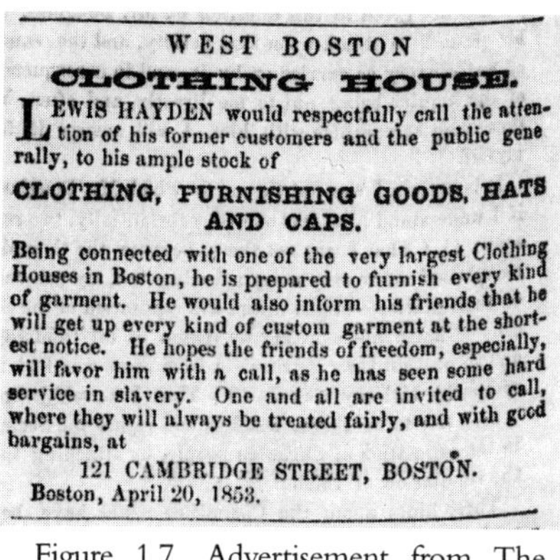

Figure 1.7 Advertisement from The Liberator, 21 April 1853. Photographed by John Seigfried; image used by permission of Mudd Library, Oberlin College.

Most of the copy is devoted to Hayden as a merchant in his primary capacity of selling things. Slavery is introduced, not through him but by reference to his customers—friends of freedom—who already know that Hayden "has seen some hard service in slavery." In the ad printed in 1854 (below) the mention of slavery has dropped out all together. (See figure 1.8.)

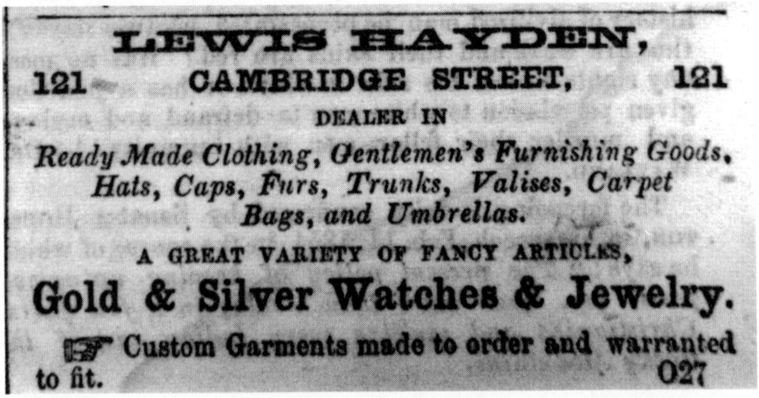

LEWIS HAYDEN,
121 CAMBRIDGE STREET, 121
DEALER IN
Ready Made Clothing, Gentlemen's Furnishing Goods, Hats, Caps, Furs, Trunks, Valises, Carpet Bags, and Umbrellas.
A GREAT VARIETY OF FANCY ARTICLES,
Gold & Silver Watches & Jewelry.
Custom Garments made to order and warranted to fit. 027

Figure 1.8 Advertisement from *The Liberator,* 5 Jan 1855. Photographed by John Seigfried; image used by permission of Mudd Library, Oberlin College.

As Hayden gained a foothold in the market, he emphasized aspects other than his racial status. Slavery—as a market lure—had done its work.

In Frank Luther Mott's view, slavery "lent itself by its very nature to magazine handling, and the question of slavery was discussed with more fervor and with more white paper and printer's ink than any other topic before the people in those days."[50] Garrison gave *The Liberator* advertisers leeway to use moral or ideological tie-ins to antislavery as their means of persuasion.[51] In doing so, Garrison recognized that reactions to slavery enabled him to adapt the existing discourse of advertising to play to emerging market demands. During the years 1850 to 1860—the same decade that saw a 100 percent increase in abolitionist publications and is seen as the golden age of slave narrative publication—the advertising section of *The Liberator* grew from a column or less on page three to several (two to four) columns on both pages three and four.[52] As the number of ads increased, so did their degree of sophistication. Rather than a simple announcement of information and goods available for sale, these products were being offered to the public as a reflection of antislavery sentiment.

Even though Garrison gave away space to the latest in medical quackery, the number of advertisements for books and other printed material far exceeds those for Dr. Porter's Anti-Scrofulous Panacea and the like.[53] The great preponderance of literary wares offered for sale in *The Liberator* suggests something about the power of narrative for Garrison's purposes. In 1851, for instance, *The Liberator* printed 13 advertisements for "medicines," while 34 separate titles were offered for sale in that same year. And, unlike advertising practices in, for example, *The Atlantic Monthly* (founded in 1857), none of the publishers of these books and magazines were affiliated with *The Liberator.* Many of the titles were advertised, however, through their connection to Garrison's cause.

IV. *The Liberator* as a Cultural Emblem of the Literary Marketplace

The ads appearing in *The Liberator* show that slavery was being used by advertisers as a successful lure for customers. The ads also tell us that while generating a new fervor over political issues, the topics of debate were calling attention to a new market for American writers, black and white. Look, for instance, at the following advertisements for books and periodicals (figure 1.9).

BOOKS

NARRATIVE of the Life of William W. Brown, a Fugitive Slave. Written by himself. Complete edition, tenth thousand. Price 25 cts.

Anti-Slavery Harp: a collection of Songs for Anti-Slavery Meetings. Compiled by Wm. W. Brown. Second edition. Price 12 1-2 cts.

Memoir of Rev. Abel Brown, by his Companion, C. S. Brown—62 1-2 cts.

Despotism in America. 4th edition—25 cts.

Archy Moore, 25 cts.

The Church as it is; or the Forlorn Hope of Slavery, by Parker Pillsbury. Second edition—revised and improved—15 cts.

History of the Mexican War; or Facts for the People, showing the relation of the United States Government to Slavery. Compiled from official and authentic Documents. By Loring Moody—20 cts.

Liberty Minstrel (Clark's) 50 cts.

Mr. Parker's Sermon of the Moral and Spiritual Condition of Boston—15 cts.

Revelations, &c. By A. J. Davis, the Clairvoyant—2 00; Davis's Chart, 1 50.

Christian Non-Resistance, by Adin Ballou—38 cts.

A Review of the Causes and Consequences of the Mexican War. By William Jay—75 cts.

The Maniac and other Poems, by George S. Burleigh—75 cts.

Charles Sumner's Oration: The True Grandeur of Nations, best edition, at the reduced price of 12 1-2 cents; and many other valuable anti-slavery Works, together with a good assortment of Books on Physiology, Phrenology, and the Water Cure.

For sale by BELA MARSH, No. 25 Cornhill.

June 15. 6mo.

Figure 1.9 Advertisement from *The Liberator,* 21 August 1851. Photographed by John Seigfried; image used by permission of Mudd Library, Oberlin College.

Headed by William Wells Brown's narrative, many of the texts advertised in this ad have some connection to abolition—whether it be descriptions of abolitionist activities, or biographies of slaves or prominent abolitionists; each text has a specific appeal to an abolitionist audience. This ad, published in 1851, predates Stowe's success with *Uncle Tom's Cabin* and distinctly demonstrates that taste for things abolitionist was already defining a market that her novel later tapped.[54] The ad notes that Brown's narrative has already sold "ten thousand," and though such assertions may not reflect the facts, the force of such a figure makes it clear that works developing an explicit connection to abolition met with success. Scrutinizing the list carefully, one can see that only those works that speak to an evangelical abolitionist audience succeed in this marketplace.

The ad merits our attention on a purely visual level as well. It departs from the conventions of advertising followed during the period by allowing the advertiser more space than the prescribed three inches. And, perhaps just as striking, is the use of type larger than agate 5 1/2 point, bold-face, all caps, and a larger border that holds it together. It would seem that Garrison, in allowing advertisers to take such liberties, was allowing them to be "as harsh as truth," and thus granting the same privileges of discourse that he, himself, found absolutely essential. In order for these products to stand up for the cause they must be able to stand out.[55]

A comparable list of books for sale printed three years later registers further developments. (See figure 1.10.) Notice that the header is distinguished by the use of the verbal expression ("has been") in the second line. Using verbs to make advertising copy more narrative did not become popular in ads until much later in the decade. Another notable aspect of this advertisement is the date of publication featured as the "header." "The Year 1853" is both the first and largest line of the advertisement, highlighting for the reader a sense of its importance. These books, the reader should think, are offered to readers as products of their time, and for their time. They urge readers to join in what is happening now by purchasing current titles. The appeal is in timeliness. Up-to-date books encourage readers to turn to the marketplace as a way to keep their morality in step with the time. Further, the copy situates these texts within abolitionist culture by claiming that they have "met with great favor." The degree of favor is here determined by the ultimate measure: "large sales." Each of the twelve books mentioned, though part of the conglomerate concept of "popular book," is individuated through the distinction of font. Typically, a promotional sentence or phrase follows up each title. Both characteristics were an advance over the sample advertisement of 1851; each title is distinguished from the next by type face and appears with a discrete pitch for its worthiness, a voucher for its popularity, or a suggestion for its use.

The Year 1853

Has been a year prolific in good Books.

John P. Jewett & Company,

Among their numerous issues, have published the following, which have met with great favor from the public, and large sales, and which should be found in every Library.

Mrs. Child's Life of Isaac T. Hopper,

One of the most intensely interesting books ever published. 10,000 copies in 4 months.

THE SHADY SIDE,

BY MRS. HUBBELL.

A thrilling tale of the vicissitudes of a country minister's life. [illegible],000 copies in 8 months.

THE MYSTERIOUS PARCHMENT

OR, SATANIC LICENSE.

A powerfully written Temperance Tale. *Fourth Thousand.*

LECTURES TO YOUNG MEN,

BY REV. RUFUS W. CLARK.

First thousand sold in four days.

Voices from the Silent Land,

OR, LEAVES OF CONSOLATION FOR THE AFFLICTED.

BY MRS. H. DWIGHT WILLIAMS.

A beautiful gift for a friend in affliction.

THE LAST HOURS OF CHRIST.

BY W. G. SCHAUFFLER, Missionary at Constantinople.

A religious work of rare excellence and beauty.

THE PERSIAN FLOWER,

Being a Memoir of a daughter of Rev. Justin Perkins, of Persia. A sweet child.

DR. E. C. ROGERS'S GREAT WORK

ON THE

Philosophy of Mysterious Agents.

The most learned and satisfactory explanation of the spirit rappings yet published.

The Writings of Prof. B. B. Edwards,

WITH A MEMOIR BY DR. PARK.

Similitudes from the Ocean and the Prairie.

BY LUCY LARCOM.

Literally, a book of gems, or string of pearls.

A SABBATH SCENE.

BY JOHN G. WHITTIER.

With thirteen Illustrations, by Billings.

THE KEY

TO

UNCLE TOM'S CABIN

A new 12mo. edition just out.

☞ 90,000 copies published of the 8vo. edition.

HINTS FOR THE HOUSEHOLD,

BY REV. WM. M. THAYER.

PICTURES AND STORIES FROM UNCLE TOM'S CABIN,

And the EDINBURGH DOLL AND OTHER TALES, for CHILDREN; being Nos. one and two of a new series of Juveniles.

NEW MUSIC BOOKS.

POLYHYMNIA, AND EUPHONIA.

The *first*, a collection of *Sacred Music*. Euphonia, a collection of Glees and part Songs. By HEUBERER and PERABEAU.

In press, to be issued in a few days, a thrilling work on the Catholic question, entitled,

THE CONVENT AND THE MANSE.

ALSO,

THE DOVECOTE;

OR, HEART OF THE HOMESTEAD.

A genuine New England Home Story.

The Boston Almanac for 1854,

AND ITS NEW COMPANION, THE

LADY'S ALMANAC.

JOHN P. JEWETT & CO. will publish the above beautiful and useful Annuals, the Boston, Dec. 15, the Lady's, Dec. 1st. A work so long and favorably known as the Boston Almanac simply needs announcing to secure its sale. This number will contain sixty new and superb engravings, twenty-four of these being the new churches of Boston built since 1842, elegantly engraved, with the usual variety of other matter. THE LADY'S ALMANAC, after the elegant style of the other, is a new claimant for public favor, which we believe it will find. It will be a most useful little pocket manual for the ladies, containing a great variety of useful receipts, bouquets of flowers, and calendar and memorandum vignettes, pages for each day and month of the year, portraits of our most distinguished female authors, hints for the toilet, numerous engravings, &c. &c.; elegantly bound in cloth, with gilt edges. Same price as the Boston Almanac. For sale by all Booksellers.

Figure 1.10 Advertisement from *The Liberator,* 13 Jan 1854. Photographed by John Seigfried; image used by permission of Mudd Library, Oberlin College.

NEW BOOKS,

OF RARE INTEREST AND VALUE,

JUST PUBLISHED BY

JOHN P. JEWETT & COMPANY,

BOSTON.

OWING to the unparalleled draft upon our resources, during the past year, on account of the unexampled sale of *Uncle Tom's Cabin*, a large number of most valuable manuscripts were obliged to lie untouched in our safe, waiting a favorable moment to appear in print. We have availed ourselves of the earliest moment, and now offer them to the *readers of good books*. Most of them are issued. Those still in press will be published speedily.

THE SHADY SIDE;

OR, LIFE IN A COUNTRY PARSONAGE,

BY A PASTOR'S WIFE.

This volume is designed, in a measure, as a contrast to that charming little book, *Sunny Side*, and we doubt not that it will meet with quite as favorable a reception as that work. It is written in an admirable style, and he who commences its perusal will hardly be able to stop until he has gone through. Price 75 cts.

Count Struensee the Skeptic, and THE CHRISTIAN.

TRANSLATED FROM THE GERMAN BY MRS. WILSON.

THE LAST HOURS OF CHRIST,

Missionary at Constantinople.

Dr. Beecher's Third Volume.

White Slavery in the Barbary States

BY HON. CHARLES SUMNER, U. S. S.

Judge Jay's Writings on Slavery,

In one volume, 12 mo., with a portrait.

Philosophy of Mysterious Rappings,

OR, THE DYNAMIC LAWS AND RELATIONS OF MAN,

THE TRIAL BY JURY,

GERMAN UNCLE TOM,

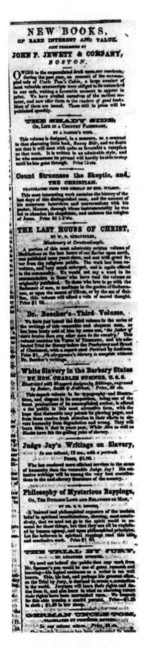

Figure 1.11 Advertisement from *The Liberator,* 15 January 1855. Photographed by John Seigfried; image used by permission of Mudd Library, Oberlin College.

The degree of actual persuasion is still minimal, especially when compared to a similar ad printed the following year in January 1855. Once again, John P. Jewett and Company offers a selection of books for sale. This time, only nine titles make up the list, and some are still, as the copy tells us, in press, but "will be published speedily." As with the books advertised in the previous example, these books are not only new, they are—or will be—hot off the press. And, in addition to the use of various fonts and print sizes, this time the publisher also includes the price of each volume as well as a short promotional paragraph detailing the special qualities of the books. Here the reader learns what the advertiser values as selling points. Rather than promote these books through sheer popularity, this advertiser rewards its customers with a compliment: if you buy these books you will exhibit your "rare interest and value"—the phrase that headlines this new list of books.

These books are presented as following in *Uncle Tom's Cabin*'s wake. Held up for publication because of *Uncle Tom's Cabin*'s unparalleled success, they—like a precious commodity—have been "stowed" in the publisher's safe. Now that the market has been primed by Stowe's novel, these texts emerge at this "favorable moment" that is defined in terms of *Uncle Tom's Cabin.* Each text relates, even if tangentially, to the subjects treated in *Uncle Tom's Cabin;* Christianity, the ministry, slavery, and spiritualism respectively, are taken up in the books offered here for sale. All of the works—like Stowe's novel—are given a decidedly nonfiction stance by emphasizing their historical sense and social accuracy regarding their topics. Presented under the rubric "antislavery literature," each work is praised for its literariness as well as its factuality, thus blurring the distinction between fiction and nonfiction. Pitched to an emerging consumer culture with a conscience, these works—even when presented as fiction—promise readers truth through the accurate reflection of the contemporary moral landscape marred by slavery.

The trend toward blending fiction and nonfiction—galvanized by the use of the slave narratives and popularized beyond a strictly abolitionist readership by Stowe—only intensified throughout this period. In a startling ad for "a history" by Charles Emory Stevens, the reader is told in bold, all caps agate type, "NO ANTI-SLAVERY NOVELS NEEDED, When the Truth is So Much Stronger and Stranger than Fiction" (see figure 1.12). This ad, like the one printed below, plays on a value judgement that fiction is sensationalistic and without inherent merit, a view that had long troubled American cultural commentators on both sides of the color line (see figure 1.13).[56] Fiction—made popular by its sentimental and sensationalistic plots of gothic novels—is supplanted by this new form of prose heralded as "stronger and stranger than fiction."

In fact, perusal of sale book lists published in *The Liberator* after 1853—in other words, after *A Key to Uncle Tom's Cabin* was published to verify, via

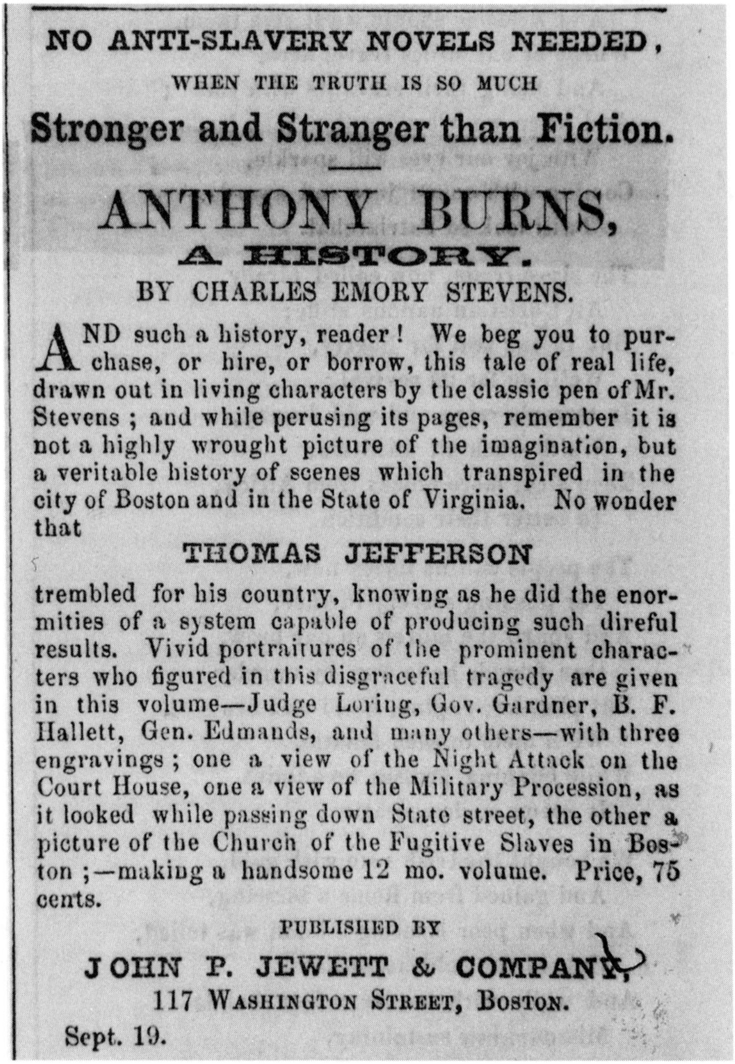

NO ANTI-SLAVERY NOVELS NEEDED,

WHEN THE TRUTH IS SO MUCH

Stronger and Stranger than Fiction.

ANTHONY BURNS,

A HISTORY.

BY CHARLES EMORY STEVENS.

AND such a history, reader! We beg you to purchase, or hire, or borrow, this tale of real life, drawn out in living characters by the classic pen of Mr. Stevens; and while perusing its pages, remember it is not a highly wrought picture of the imagination, but a veritable history of scenes which transpired in the city of Boston and in the State of Virginia. No wonder that

THOMAS JEFFERSON

trembled for his country, knowing as he did the enormities of a system capable of producing such direful results. Vivid portraitures of the prominent characters who figured in this disgraceful tragedy are given in this volume—Judge Loring, Gov. Gardner, B. F. Hallett, Gen. Edmands, and many others—with three engravings; one a view of the Night Attack on the Court House, one a view of the Military Procession, as it looked while passing down State street, the other a picture of the Church of the Fugitive Slaves in Boston;—making a handsome 12 mo. volume. Price, 75 cents.

PUBLISHED BY

JOHN P. JEWETT & COMPANY,

117 WASHINGTON STREET, BOSTON.

Sept. 19.

Figure 1.12 Advertisement from *The Liberator,* 3 Oct 1856. Photographed by John Seigfried; image used by permission of Mudd Library, Oberlin College.

available slave testimony, the novel's "facts"—show that a taste for the real clearly pervades the language of the literary marketplace. The language used to sell these books is unique to *The Liberator* and thus is suggestive of the paper's formative power.

Startling Disclosures!

Truth Stranger than Fiction.

AN INSIDE VIEW

—OF—

SLAVERY;

—OR—

A TOUR AMONG THE PLANTERS.

BY C. G. PARSONS, M. D.

THIS is not a romance, but a true record of facts, seen and heard during an extensive tour through the Southern States, by an intelligent Physician. It is truly an extraordinary volume. Those who believe that the system of Slavery has been caricatured in the novels of the day, would do well to sit down to a calm and dispassionate perusal of these FACTS from real life.

JUST PUBLISHED BY

JOHN P. JEWETT & CO.,

117 WASHINGTON STREET,

Oct. 12. 4w BOSTON.

CORA AND THE DOCTOR:

—OR—

REVELATIONS

—OF A—

PHYSICIAN'S WIFE.

AGREEABLY to promise, we opened a 'new vein' on the 18th of September, and 2000 lbs. of the richest ore were taken from it on the first day; since which time we have found it impossible to supply the demand.

CORA AND THE DOCTOR will be, as we predicted, a book of mark. The fourth thousand is now ready. The reviewers are delighted with it. Read what they say:—

A story which displays great skill and good taste in the writer. [Daily Advertiser, Boston.

It has rarely been our lot to peruse a more intensely interesting book than this—[Wesleyan Journal.

Our heart has been made to throb with its dramatic incidents, and our eyes to well up with the pathos of its heart-revealings.—[McMakin's Courier, Phila.

One of the most interesting volumes that has lately been issued from the American press.—[Boston Herald.

A charmingly written volume, which will amply repay perusal.—[Daily British Whig, Canada.

The fragrance it leaves behind is pure and refreshing.—[Christian Mirror, Portland.

If our judgment is not greatly at fault, Cora and The Doctor will prove to be one of the most popular stories of the season.—[N. E. Farmer.

It is indeed a book of power, poetry, elegance, and Christian sentiments—one among thousands.—[Evening Transcript, Boston.

PUBLISHED BY

JOHN P. JEWETT & CO.,

117 WASHINGTON STREET,

Oct. 12. 4w BOSTON.

PASSMORE WILLIAMSON

IN MOYAMENSING JAIL.

JUST PUBLISHED,

A FINE Portrait representing this *Martyr to the cause of Freedom, Truth and Justice*, (versus LAW,) taken from life, in the cell in which he has been incarcerated by Judge Kane for alleged Contempt of Court. Size of the Picture, 16 by 20 in. Price, Fifty Cents.

Those desiring early impressions of this interesting Picture can receive them by leaving their names with the Publisher, THOMAS CURTIS, 134 Arch street, Philadelphia, where all orders for the trade must be addressed.

Philadelphia, Sept. 20, 1855.

Worcester Hydropathic Institution.

THE Proprietors of this Institution aim to make it a comfortable home for invalids at all seasons. The location is elevated and healthy, yet easy of access from all parts of the city. For particulars, address S. ROGERS, M. D., or E. F. ROGERS, Sup't, Worcester, Mass.

Worcester, April 13.

Figure 1.13 Advertisement from *The Liberator,* 12 Oct 1855. Photographed by John Seigfried; image used by permission of Mudd Library, Oberlin College.

From its inception, *The Liberator* pressed its readers toward what Karen Sanchez-Eppler has called "moments of identification," by establishing parallels between the readership and the slave population Garrison wished to free.[57] He justified his need to be "as harsh as truth," by likening the ravages experienced by the slave family to a white family trapped in a burning house. Garrison invaded his readers' security through his use of humanitarian realism, conjuring fearful images of bodily harm. He thus used reader anxiety as a political tool. "No! no!" Garrison exclaims: "Tell a man whose house is on fire to give a moderate alarm; tell him to moderately rescue his wife from the hands of the ravisher; tell the mother to gradually extricate her babe from the fire into which it has fallen;—but urge me not to use moderation in a cause like the present."[58] As with the motto, "Am I not a Man and a Brother" used by abolitionists internationally, the use of socially defined and accepted relationships—and in particular, the family bond—encourages reader identification and responsibility. The reader's anxiety level rises as she or he further recognizes the peril black bodies encounter through institutionalized slavery because Garrison here likens slavery to a raging fire consuming the house and its inhabitants. Invoking the "humanitarian narrative," Garrison depends on the link between the body's discomfort and wrongdoing.[59] His very graphic language works as a goad, urging readers to allay their anxiety through immediate action (an important contrast to the gradualism of other abolitionists) as they heed his message. The ads under consideration here, and the books they are meant to promote, are the descendents of Garrison's incendiary language.

Designed to agitate readers through their abandonment of the decorum that ruled ordinary discourse of the period, ads boasted that books now made "disclosures" that will be either "startling" or "astounding" to the contemporary reader (see figure 1.13). They use methods of discourse that are *real,* as defined by Garrison in his inaugural address to readers of *The Liberator* in 1831. Rather than novelized versions of the truth, these works resemble the slave narratives that also appeared in the pages of *The Liberator.* They provide "revelations" and will help "indoctrinate the children" against the evils of slavery—a notion that has also been made *real* through consistent appeal to parallel experiences of nonslaves (see figure 1.11). In his promotion of abolition, Garrison, and others like him, cleared the way for a new literary sensibility—one that adopted a manner as "harsh as truth" in part as a way to educate the reading public about the social ills of slavery and other systematic injustices.

What is most striking about the book announcements is the way characteristics specific to the slave narratives now define the literary standards of this period for those committed to abolition. The taste for veracity had noticeably increased around the issue of slave narratives. Prefaces and reviews of the narratives, as well as the narrators themselves, always provided verifiable details to satisfy the demand, not just for verisimilitude, but for true experience. The narratives' double purpose—as political tool and art form—would only be accomplished if they were both free of doubt as to their truth and exciting as stories. Taken together, these two qualities constituted "realness." The ads and the texts they represent indicate that the construction of the real was inseparable from the ideological purposes it was designed to serve.

Part of how "realness" was put across to the reader involved what one reviewer called "artlessness," a quality Harriet Beecher Stowe boasted of when she claimed that God wrote *Uncle Tom's Cabin.*[60] The reviewer who praised Henry Bibb's narrative as "an unvarnished tale,"[61] could just as easily have been writing advertising copy for *Cora and the Doctor* (see figure 1.13).[62] The emphasis on the homespun and ordinary nature of the books advertised in the pages of *The Liberator* is consistent with the popular interest in slave narratives, for both their political reasons and entertainment value. For, as Ann Fabian notes, "in this sense the antislavery movement, so full of high purpose, also offered entertainment. Former slaves who told their stories attracted crowds."[63] Former slaves who sold their stories also made money.

Presented as a market phenomenon, texts written by former slaves such as Frederick Douglass's *My Bondage and My Freedom,* were advertised in terms of their popularity. The fact that they were so popular provides us with a verifiable link between the evangelical abolitionism of the era and its commitment to reform.

The advertising copy (see figure 1.14) illustrates that an attempt to delineate popular taste is made. And the first selling point is the simple fact that Douglass' text has a "natural" market in the United States because "it is the work of an American slave." *Putnam Monthly*'s reviewer of Frederick Douglass's *Life and Bondage* published in 1854, admitted that readers "have read it with the unbroken attention with which we absorbed *Uncle Tom's Cabin.*"[64] What the advertisers don't mention is that authentic experience costs more. Douglass's book costs a whopping $1.25 as compared with the average price of the other books here advertised: a mere $.75. Clearly, "realness" was something that not only sold but also paid, and this fact is reflected in the rising number of advertisements for literary culture in *The Liberator.* By emphasizing the "real," print mediated the social consciousness of reality from an abolitionist perspective—a perspective that held sway in the literary marketplace of the period.

The Liberator's ability to survive was a direct result of its innovative use of advertising and shows how Garrison turned to the marketplace as both a source of revenue and a medium for the cause. Indeed, every aspect of *The*

5000 Copies Sold in Two Days,

OF

My Bondage and My Freedom,

BY FREDERICK DOUGLASS.

One Vol., 12mo., 464 pp., Illustrated. Price, $1.25.

WHY SO POPULAR?

It is the Work of an American Slave,
Therefore excites American Sympathy!
Every line and letter are his own,
And it is a Volume of Truth and Power!
It tells the earnest, startling truth,
Without ranting or madness!
It addresses the intellect and the heart!
Every free Press chants its praise,
Every free Voter will read it,
And every Bookseller supply it.

MILLER, ORTON & MULLIGAN, *Publishers*,
25 Park Row, New York, and 107 Genesee st., Auburn.

Figure 1.14 Advertisement from *The Liberator,* 24 August 1855. Photographed by John Seigfried; image used by permission of Mudd Library, Oberlin College.

Liberator—from articles and letters-to-the editor to advertisements and announcements—shaped the reader's response to abolition. To drive the cause even further, Garrison departed from nineteenth-century periodical publishing practices. The newspaper violated rules governing the decorum of print culture, including the standards in typography and sales pitch, in order to promote both the message and the messenger.

The development of Garrisonian abolitionism as a commercial enterprise and the terms Garrison used to pitch its wares, literary and otherwise, are suggestive in their concurrence. The public debates over slavery encouraged in the pages of *The Liberator* coalesced with a new trend in literary taste, one that significantly blurred the distinction between fiction and fact and led the way toward realism. And this new mixture of story and history, in turn, corresponded to a new literary genre—one that was developed and maintained by the forces of Garrisonian abolition. Protorealist in style, many of the works advertised in *The Liberator* make use of a strong association between slavery as an institution and the lived experience of all people—an association that would eventually become a narrative feature of many important works. Further evidence of this connection can be found in fictional works such as William Wells Brown's *Clotel* (1853), Harriet Beecher Stowe's *Dred* (1856) and Herman Melville's "Benito Cereno" (1856). Thus "truth stronger and stranger than fiction," a slogan proclaimed by Garrison, epitomizes Garrisonian advertising practices while also indicating new trends in literary tastes and the market for them.

Making it Real

The Impact of Slave Narratives on the Literary Marketplace[1]

Whether as propaganda for abolition or an art form in their own right, the political and rhetorical power of slave narratives cannot be exaggerated.[2] Nor can the link between their popularity and their influence on the development of U.S. literature be ignored.[3] The vast number of slave narratives published testifies to their marketability, as do the numbers of imposter and "crossover" works written by white or nonslave writers. The numerous editions individual works saw indicates the degree to which certain narratives succeeded in the literary marketplace. Frederick Douglass's 1845 narrative sold four editions in its first year and the first edition sold out.[4] Yet discussions of the narratives tend to develop their social, political, and literary value without giving full consideration to them as market phenomenon.

This chapter treats slave narratives as an important market force, situating them as a tap root for what will ultimately become "realism" in the United States. But in order to uncover this historical connection, first we must establish both the prominence of slave narratives and their literary strategies. Ultimately, this analysis will challenge the use of Frederick Douglass's 1845 narrative as a definitive model for the genre itself by exploring the use of finances as a tool to garner reader sympathy in less prominent authors of the genre. The frequent use of money as an index for personal affliction dovetails with realism's penchant for finances. Human suffering, translated into economic terms, forms the central link between the "humanitarian narrative" of the slave narratives and the humanitarian realism that is the genre's legacy.

I. Slave Narratives: Frederick Douglass and the Marketplace

Frederick Douglass's 1845 narrative has been used most widely as a model of the "slave narrative" genre and thus, as a highpoint of an emerging literary tradition. As a result, today's readers encounter his first narrative, published by William Lloyd Garrison, with well-deserved awe. Douglass's text remains a marvel of rhetorical mastery as well as of philosophical depth. However, the appreciation of Douglass's narrative primarily in terms of its literary accomplishments has impeded our ability to recognize the impact that Douglass and countless other writers in this genre had on the emerging literary marketplace and on realism in its nascent form.

Douglass's first narrative not only went through many successive editions, but, over time, he expanded and republished his story several times. *My Bondage and My Freedom* is his 1855 version.[5] By 1881, he filled out his story further and titled it *The Life and Times of Frederick Douglass, Written by Himself.* Part of what is interesting about Douglass's publishing history is that he, like many of his fellow slave narrators, managed to play international copyright to his advantage. He published books in Ireland, England, France, and Germany, while also garnering royalties. Consequently, Douglass handled the literary marketplace with a degree of canniness that eluded many white mainstream authors.[6] Thus, Douglass's success is notable for its amplitude as well as its chronological place in the history of the book in the United States. The success of his books, like the success of many other works in the genre, must have been obvious to those in the profession, if not in general.

The money and prominence Douglass earned—through book sales, lecture tours and fund raising—certainly did not elude Garrison.[7] Soon, Douglass tired of working for the cause under the direction of Garrison and other Boston-based abolitionists. The break in the relationship between Douglass and Garrison, at least in part, resulted from Garrison's realization that Douglass wasn't just a fellow abolitionist, he was also a competitor.

As time passed, Douglass became increasingly savvy about his value in the abolitionist market, ruffling feathers with demands that he be paid more as a speaker and writer for the cause because of his skill and intrinsic value as a black man and former slave. He wryly commented on the pros and cons of the marketplace for blacks in England, noting in a letter to the white abolitionist Francis Jackson, "It is quite an advantage to be a n——r here. I find I am hardly black enough for British taste, but by keeping my hair as wooly as possible I make out to pass for at least half a Negro at any rate."[8] He clearly found the function of representing his race to whites degrading, resorting to the epithet, "n——r," rather than using the term "negro" as was common among abolitionists.

His remark also shows a degree of self-conscious marketing reflected in later actions. Douglass finally tired of working for the cause as its representative "n——r," and set out to start his first paper in a series of newspapers in Rochester, New York. Though his departure from the Garrisonians captures the degree to which he was unwilling to be manipulated by whites, his remark to Jackson shows an important awareness of his market value or "advantage" as a black man in a white world. With funds raised in England and with the support of Harriet Beecher Stowe among others, Douglass broke out on his own and became a professional author as well as a famous orator and minister. He moved to Rochester where he started his newspaper, *The North Star,* in 1847. He went on to publish several important autobiographical works and numerous political speeches, maintaining an important presence in print for the rest of his life.

Sojourner Truth was inspired to begin dictating her narrative to Olive Gilbert by Douglass's success in 1845 with his first narrative.[9] And like Douglass, Truth's narrative enjoyed brisk sales through many editions.[10] After its 1850 publication, Truth purchased her first house with profits from book sales.[11] Prominently placed on the green paper cover of that first edition are the words, "WITH A PORTRAIT."

Six out of ten slave narratives published in the United States between 1845 and 1870 provided a portrait of the author as a frontispiece.[12] These portraits served two important functions. First of all, they offered one of many proofs that the author was REAL and in this case that means: *really* black. Yet portraits were no guarantee of textual authenticity.

The portrait of the author functions as a central textual element—one used to produce the black body with the black text, as Robert Stepto has argued.[13] But, at the same time, such portraits also help heighten the effect of the humanitarian narrative put forward by the text by invoking individual identity. Locating the author as a physical body helps foster the reader empathy unfolding text requires. In order to be successful, these texts must identify the author as a subject whose suffering is not just plausible (as in the fictional setting) but *real.*

The author portrait serves another important function: to identify and mark the former slave as *author.* Such portraits contextualize the writer in the tradition of writers whose portraits—from Byron's famous open-collared portrait on—pressed upon the volume the *seal* of authorship. Thus the necessity of the portrait to verify the writer's racial status also conferred the status of authorship that was typically reserved for more celebrated figures such as Lowell, Longfellow, Stowe, and even Garrison, whose portraits were sold separately and as accompaniments to their works.

Figure 2.1 William Wells Brown Frontispiece with signature. Photograph courtesy of The Library Company of Philadelphia.

We might turn to William Wells Brown's career for a glimpse at the creation of author-as-celebrity model of black authorship in the contemporary marketplace. Like Douglass, Brown was enormously successful as an author. His *Narrative of William W. Brown, A Fugitive Slave. Written by Himself* (1847) sold 8000 copies within two years.[14] Assuming that Brown made 25 cents per copy sold by 1850, he made $4,500 and the book was going into its third edition. In today's currency that figure roughly translates to $75,000.[15]

But what qualifies Brown as a model of authorship for this study is the fact that he extended the genre limitations placed on black authors. He successfully published in a variety of forms and was the first black man to get a novel published in the United States. *Clotel,* a novelized version of the Thomas Jefferson and Sally Hemings affair, saw several editions. Brown did not stop with these works. As we saw in the advertisement for books published by J. P. Jewett in *The Liberator,* he also sold anthologies and other materials promoted by the association with his name and identity. Furthermore, he pursued separate genres as a slave narrator, novelist, dramatist, and historian, bringing out ten full-length works before his death in 1874. Brown's success is also reflected in the portraits reproduced in his volumes.

Particularly striking is the frontispiece of his 1855 publication, *The American Fugitive in Europe: Sketches of Places and People Abroad,* by J. P. Jewett, one of the premiere publishing houses in Boston (see figure 2.1).

Here readers come face to face with the eager and intent glance of the author. The realism of the portrait sets it off from the other slave narrators as well as white, mainstream authors. The fineness of detail in his hair, for instance, makes an immediate impression on viewers, as would the angle of his jaw line and the alert look in his eyes.[16] But perhaps what is most striking about the portrait is the presence of Brown's signature directly below it. Among slave narratives, the signature asserts Brown's literacy. Within the context of the history of authorship, the signature calls attention to his status as not just the author of this work, but as an author within the larger context of mainstream culture. In fact, author signatures were soon to become a kind of trademark. Publications by both Twain and Howells brandished the author's signature across the front boards of their books.

With the appearance of the author's signature as part of the frontispiece, the slave narrator moves from the position of emergent culture to the level of the dominant culture.[17] The signature asserts a crucial sense of agency in the production of the slave narrative as a literary text. An emblem of the literacy that has been so closely linked with freedom, the signature also lays claim to literacy. Just as "written by him/herself" became a trademark of the genre, a printed signature was the mark of successful authorship. In the

JAMES WILLIAMS.

Figure 2.2 James Williams. Photograph courtesy of The Library Company of Philadelphia.

signed frontispiece to the slave narratives, we have visual evidence of the slave narrator transformed into successful author through publication.

Imposter narratives with accompanying portraits did circulate and were outed to the public in announcements that appeared in newspapers such as *The Liberator.* Perhaps one of the most embarrassing cases for the abolition movement itself was that of James Williams, an African American who published a "slave narrative" in the 1830s (see figure 2.2).

As it turns out, *The Authentic Narrative of James Williams, An American Slave* is not "authentic" at all. Though "dictated" to the abolitionist and poet John Greenleaf Whittier, it is a work of fiction. Williams was not a slave, but a writer savvy enough to realize that this genre was the one with the most currency, especially for a black man.[18] These facts, coupled with the general function of the author's portrait at large, must have resonated deeply in the consciousness of both producers and consumers of the genre. Indeed, Douglass' remarks about the use of his racial status resonate here as well. In the case of Williams—he was black, but not a slave; the rejection of his book because of the possibility that it was fiction rather than fact makes it clear that to make it in this marketplace, these two pieces of identity interlock to form the only model for black authorship.[19]

II. Truth Stronger Than Fiction: And Truth Sells!

The self-conscious recognition of the marketability of slave narratives became a prominent theme of the narratives. Indeed, many of the slave narrators make their success as authors and speakers central to their stories. Josiah Henson, the author of *Truth Stranger and Stronger than Fiction,* converted the 76-page pamphlet he had published in 1849 called "The Life of Josiah Henson: Formerly a slave, now an inhabitant of Canada" into a 240-page book. His title for the longer work—*Truth Stronger than Fiction, Father Henson's Story of His Own Life*—vies with Stowe's fictionalized treatment and even reproaches her use of *his* story.[20] He asserts his superiority to Stowe's "fiction" in the claim to "truth" in his title while also emphasizing his ownership of the story through the use of the emphatic "own." Thus, despite Stowe's introduction (which serves as her de facto authorization) of Henson's text, the title lays claim to his life as *his* to commodify through publication. The frontispiece furthers this impression by presenting Henson proudly situated atop his signature (see figure 2.3).

What Stowe's introduction calls attention to most is the active marketplace for writing that pertains to slavery. Inviting a comparison to other works in circulation, Stowe writes, "Among all the singular and interesting records to which the institution of American slavery has given rise, we know of none more striking, more characteristic and instructive, than that of Josiah Henson."[21] Stowe's comments make a claim not only for the originality of Henson's work, but also for its literariness by foregrounding the text as "striking." But lest the text be mistaken as a work with literary intentions solely, Stowe hastens to inform readers of Henson's purpose: "Our excellent friend," she explains, "has prepared this edition of his works

Josiah Henson

Figure 2.3 Josiah Henson. Photograph Courtesy of The Library Company of Philadelphia.

for the purpose of redeeming from slavery a beloved brother, who has groaned for many years under the yoke of a hard master."[22] His chances of achieving this goal are good; we learn from Henson that the first edition of his narrative sold 2,000 copies,[23] and that prior to preparing the manuscript for publication he raised over $17,000.[24] In today's currency, that is well over a quarter of a million dollars.[25]

Henson's success and his incorporation of it into his story typifies the genre to an extent that scholars have not entirely recognized. As Henry Louis Gates, Jr. has noted, the work exhibits "a general stress on the material level of existence or indeed of subsistence, sordid facts, hunger, money."[26] And it is precisely the stress on the material facts of survival that Henson urges on his readers at the start. But Douglass's narrative is an important exception to this trend. This stylistic feature of Douglass's narrative might also help explain why the material success of the slave narratives has been omitted in the study of authorship in the United States.

Nary a word about his finances enters Douglass's 1845 *Narrative* with the one brief exception of his mention of unfair wages while he was working in Baltimore. Indeed, this may be one of the many reasons his text succeeded canonically while others like it failed. By steering clear of the capitalism fueling the abolitionist movement, Douglass's text protects it from the taint of money. His focus on the moral turpitude of slavery and not his need to profit from the sale of his books corresponds closely to the approach those linked with abolition favored. Furthermore, his silence about money keeps the focus on the morality of abolition and emancipation and thus circumvents the debate over wage slavery running rampant at the time.[27] For instance, Abner Kneeland—a leader of a radical labor movement and later editor and publisher of the *Boston Investigator*—offered Garrison his meeting room to denounce the American Colonization Society on 15 October 1830 when no other society or organization would open its doors.[28] Ultimately Garrison sought to distance himself from the worker movement as its purposes turned to reforms in labor not morality.[29]

We might also see Douglass's refusal to be bought out of slavery as another reason that his image was purified among abolitionists who sought to disassociate the movement from capital. His insistence—until he saw that living abroad was not truly possible for his wife and children—that the slave owner be denied compensation as his freedom was both natural and inalienable, was a radical expression of the moral high ground claimed by the abolitionists. The canonization of his 1845 narrative maintains that moral high ground and thus speaks more to the cultural and political needs of the movement itself. The use of Douglass's text as an emblem for the genre of the slave narrative does not, however, do justice to the genre's impact on the dominant literary forms of the day and on the development of

REV. NOAH DAVIS,
PASTOR OF THE
Saratoga Street African Baptist Church,
BALTIMORE.

Figure 2.4 Reverend Noah Davis. Photograph Courtesy of The Library Company of Philadelphia.

realism in particular. By looking closely at those narratives that were popular but have not been canonized, we will be able to recognize the link between slave narratives and what would become literary realism through the emphasis both forms place on the importance of the marketplace in alleviating human suffering.

Noah Davis, a former slave, explained his sense of the marketplace directly to the reader in the "Notice to the Public," in which he appeals for the readers to "aid him in the sale of this book."[30] Enacting that important link between "men and things" that Booker T. Washington would urge on his readers 42 years later with the publication of his *Up From Slavery* (1901), Davis tells his tale through explicit references to money and other forms of material.

Foregrounding his financial need and narrative purpose, he reached for the uppercase in his "Notice," to ensure that the reader recognized the economic factors prompting his tale. He provides a full account of what he did with the money earned so far—including buying his family out of slavery at a cost of over $4,000.[31] We soon learn, after perusing a portrait of the author, that the funds Reverend Davis is seeking are to erect a handsome church, pictured on the next page and estimated to cost $18,000 (see figures 2.4 and 2.5).[32] Thus, Davis's expectations have a significant basis in reality; we can assume that sales would eventually generate enough revenue to put him in sight of his goal. In the meantime, he put his goal in sight of the reader:

THE SARATOGA STREET

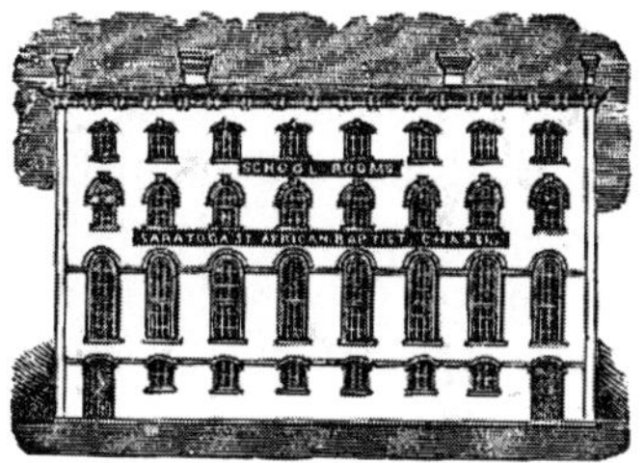

AFRICAN BAPTIST CHAPEL.

The building, of which the above cut is an imperfect representation, fronts as above 100 feet on Saratoga street, and 46 feet on Calvert street. The house is of brick, and cost over $18,000.—(See page 45.)

Figure 2.5 Noah Davis's proposed church. Photograph Courtesy of The Library Company of Philadelphia.

In a sermon he appends to the book, Davis chooses this passage from the bible as his text: "But if any provide not for his own, and especially for those of his own house, he hath denied the faith, and is worse than an infidel."[33] Davis made this biblical text a context for his canny use of the marketplace in the service of his vocation. He thus layers his purposes with those of the evangelical, reform-minded, liberal capitalists who will buy his book and help him achieve his goals.

Yet, by using the biblical passage to underwrite the commercial goals of the book rather than the moral ones, Davis breaks with the standards we find in Douglass. Indeed, literary analysis of slave narratives that were as popular as Douglass's suggests a different set of regulations and practices guiding them as literary works. These departures from Douglass show us that the genre was defined differently at the time than it has been retroactively. These works offer us an important link to the dominant literary form of realism emerging at the time.

Davis's use of money as a prominent signifier in his text stands for more than the "linguistic demonstrations of realism" William Andrews has associated with references to materiality in slave narratives. Monetary figures serve as explicit references to the material costs of the escape from slavery; life in the free world imbricates slavery and freedom within the context of capitalism. These references provide an alternate definition of freedom as a lived experience—one in need of the material forms of support sought through the practical use of publishing as a means to make a living. Or, as Davis announces to his readers on his title page, his work is "printed solely for the author's benefit."[34]

Writing as a means of making a living, a new form of the mendicant narrative popular in colonial America, was consistently an incentive to publication.[35] Writers registered that incentive directly in their literary productions. For instance, one black author, Elleanor Eldridge, published two books, both for the sole purpose of garnering revenue. Listed in the *Dictionary of American Negro Bibliography* as a "skilled servant and business woman," Eldridge details in her story the growth and subsequent loss of her real estate empire. Remarkable in part because her books are among the few written and published by a free black, she also makes use of explicit sums throughout the course of her narrative. Beginning with the 25 cents a week she earned doing a neighbor's wash and ending up with a parcel of real estate valued at $4,000, hers is a story told in very real terms. Indeed, money is not merely central to her story; it is the very reason she is writing it.[36] The first book, *Memoirs of Elleanor Eldridge,* was published in Providence in 1838 to help her raise funds necessary to prevent a threatened swindle to take over her land. Currently held in the Boston Public Library's collection as a gift from Wendell Phillips's collection in 1882, Eldridge's first book was so successful at raising funds that the same publishers put out her second volume, this one matter-of-factly titled *Elleanor's Second Book,* in 1847. It, too, was purchased by Wendell Phillips, evidence of Eldridge's favorable use of the humanitarian narrative to support herself.

Elleanor Eldridge.

Figure 2.6 Portrait of Elleanor Eldridge. Photograph courtesy of The Library Company of Philadelphia.

Like so many of the books written by blacks (and whites), both of Eldridge's books bear a portrait of the author (see figure 2.6). Yet, Eldridge's books provide an important difference from the majority of works published by blacks. Eldridge is a free black—not a slave—and thus her books offer us the exception that proves the rule. Her use of publishing as a means of gaining revenue and the inclusion of a portrait to support the enterprise makes a convincing case for race as a significant market lure. The fluid lines of her portrait depict her within the context of her need to make a living. Holding a long-handled broom rather daintily, she appears ready and able to do the work that buying her narrative will enable. Opportunity, in other words, for a black author, can be measured through book sales.

But perhaps even more striking than either Eldridge or Davis for its open engagement with the marketplace is the narrative written by Thomas H. Jones (see figure 2.7). Not included among those writers William Andrews has termed "bourgeois" for their faith in the Protestant work ethic and middle-class values, Jones' text might help us reconsider Venture Smith, Lundsford Lane, Moses Grandy, Austin Steward, and Israel Campbell. More than most black memoirists, however, these men concentrate on economic success as a primary basis on which their readers might empathize with and respect them.[37] First published in 1849, Jones titled his 46-page narrative "The Experience of Thomas H. Jones Who Was a Slave for Forty-three Years."

At least eleven different printings under this title appeared during Jones's lifetime. Throughout the course of his story, Jones makes a point of recounting his struggle in financial terms. Presenting himself as "a suffering brother" in his preface, he markets his book through the moral consumerism characteristic of the age.[38] There he urges readers through his scribe "to buy it and read it for, in doing so, you will help one of need of your sympathy and aid, and you will receive, in the perusal of this simple narrative, a more fervent conviction of the necessity and blessedness of toiling for the desolate members of the one great brotherhood who now suffers and dies, ignorant and despairing, in the fast prison land of the South."[39] In the preface, Jones makes the terms of the trade clear: purchase *and* perusal will strengthen the reader's moral conviction.

Throughout the narrative he provides concrete figures to record his struggle, using this accounting as a way to tell his story. First, a friend lent him five dollars, later he records payments he received for lectures and public appearances: $3.53 from Bethel church, $2.33 from another congregation he addressed. Rather than round off figures, he records them to the penny, registering through these accounts the precise cost of freedom in his personal finances. The insertion of material contexts—most notably money—into slave narratives emphasizes what John Ashworth has described as the interdependence of ideas and material forces.[40] History has

THE EXPERIENCE

OF

THOMAS H. JONES,

WHO WAS

A SLAVE

FOR FORTY-THREE YEARS.

Figure 2.7 Thomas H. Jones portrait. Photograph courtesy of The Library Company of Philadelphia.

rendered this emphasis unappealing, severing the material goals of capitalist liberalism from the reform movements of the nineteenth century and of abolition in particular. A rereading of the slave narratives with the developing literary marketplace in mind reestablishes this important link.

We can gain insight into how powerful an emphasis on the material might have been to a reading audience through a pirated version of Jones's narrative. The story was picked up by a printer in Boston in the late 1850s—in other words while Jones was selling his real version, there was also a fake one available. Published as *The Experience of Uncle Tom Jones,* the publication caricatured Jones's narrative for a popular, racist audience. Coupled with a segment from a novel written by a white author, the book offered both pieces as "nonfiction" work in the "slave narrative" genre. Just as in Jones's authorized publication of his story, this volume carries a portrait of the author—in cameo—on the front cover.

However, in place of the dignified portrait of the author figured in the original is a gross stereotype. Featured in this bogus printing of Jones's story, attractively packaged in bright blue-colored boards, is a caricature of Jones as the happy darky (see figure 2.8). Postured more than posed, this portrait imbues the humble Jones with pretension. The elegant hat, smoking pipe, and gloved hand resting on his breast à la Napoleon, presents Jones as a man made rich and pompous through authorship—not the "suffering brother" of his original publication. Perhaps the most striking example of how this publisher converted Jones's freedom narrative into a conventional adventure story, gotten up in the garb of race, is what was left out in order to achieve this transformation.

The story has been cut down—almost in half. Most of what had been left out concerned the financial aspect of the narrative. In other words, the very guts of the narrative have been removed. Jones had used figures and letters pertaining to the financial end of his journey from slavery to freedom as key signifiers—references to material contexts that would lend the narrative a form of reality that white readers would surely understand. Without that explicit unit of measure, Jones's story loses the power of the humanitarian narrative to invoke social justice. *The Experience of Uncle Tom Jones* loses all of its strength and much of its realism.

Recovering the dynamic use of money as a potent signifier in the slave narrative genre helps us recognize a thematic connection between slave narratives and the emerging genre of realism. And as the bastardized version of Jones's story suggests, leaving out the gritty financial facts turned a struggle for life and limb into just another adventure story. Many of realism's most important works delve deeply into the mechanics of the marketplace and its impact on the lives of its characters. For instance, in a breakthrough moment in realism, William Dean Howells barraged readers

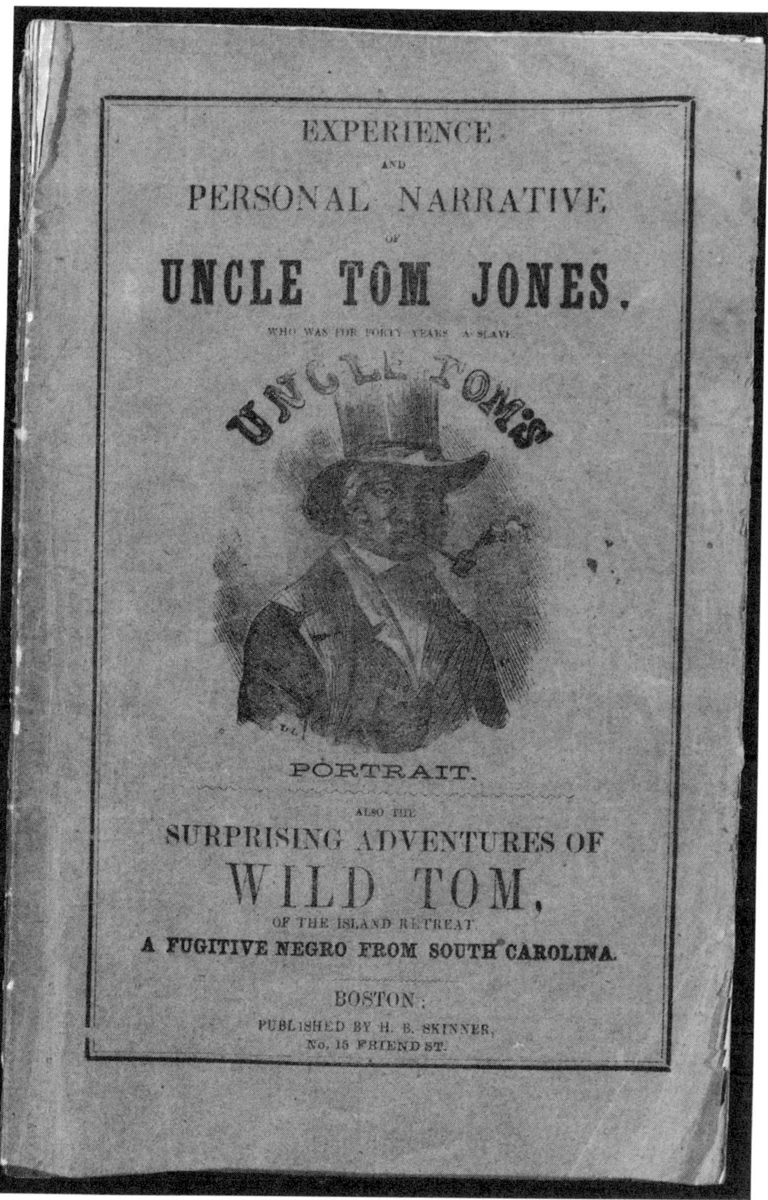
EXPERIENCE
AND
PERSONAL NARRATIVE
OF
UNCLE TOM JONES.
WHO WAS FOR FORTY YEARS A SLAVE.
UNCLE TOM'S
PORTRAIT.
ALSO THE
SURPRISING ADVENTURES OF
WILD TOM,
OF THE ISLAND RETREAT.
A FUGITIVE NEGRO FROM SOUTH CAROLINA.
BOSTON:
PUBLISHED BY H. B. SKINNER,
No. 15 FRIEND ST.

Figure 2.8 Cover of The Experience of Uncle Tom Jones. Photograph courtesy of The Library Company of Philadelphia.

with the costs and compromises of finding an apartment in New York as a way to connect with readers. Seeing it all in dollars and cents made the move his characters were undertaking—for a job—real in readers' eyes. Howells and other realists figured money was something all Americans had in common and so used it as a way to place emphasis on human experience within a social context. Realizing the enormous success of the slave narratives gives us a context for the appropriation of the theme by budding realists in the United States.

III. From "Sambo's Woes" to "Startling Disclosures!": Soaring New Trends in the Literary Marketplace

Imagine, for a moment, that you are a struggling (most likely white) writer, hamstrung by copyright laws that make publishing a very tricky business. Competition is fierce and pay is low, but you want to be a writer. As you struggle to develop your craft and make your contribution to this new nation's national literature, prominent figures among the literary gatekeepers in Boston—then the publishing center of the country—greet the work of the slave narratives as did Theodore Parker, calling them the country's "first indigenous literature." These writings—tracing the trials suffered and surmounted by the authors themselves—popularized a taste for the real by forging a connection between story and storyteller in new ways. Their popularity and freshness prompted anger among the frustrated ranks of professional authors. One such writer complained, "the shelves of book sellers groan under the weight of Sambo's woes, done up in boards."[41] Looking back through a comparison of writers like the one responsible for this complaint will help show how writers adapted their anger and anxiety over the literary success of slave narratives into viable materials for a competitive marketplace.

The reading public seemed to have an insatiable appetite for "Sambo's woes." Many slave narratives saw multiple editions while the works we now consider canonical barely sold at all. We can gauge their popularity by comparing the publication history of a slave narrative and a work by a canonized author as Frances Smith Foster has done in comparing Josiah Henson's 1849 narrative with Thoreau's *Week on the Concord and Merrimack Rivers* published in the same year. In four years, Thoreau's book sold 219 copies to Henson's 6,000.[42] As Foster concludes, "the contemporary audiences of Douglass, Brown, and Henson were far larger than those of [Thoreau, Melville, or Hawthorne] three of the literary figures most revered today."[43] Statistics like these prompt the question: How might have the popularity of slave narratives impacted the developing field of American authorship? But I'm not sure that comparisons of slave narratives to canonical texts actually help answer such a question.

Novelists who were advertised in the pages of *The Liberator* share what we would call a market niche and thus provide an "apple to apple" comparison for this study.[44] Take a writer such as Harriet Newell Baker (1815–1893). Writing under the pseudonym Madeline Leslie, she was the author of *Cora and the Doctor.* Leslie's novel was first published in 1855 by the prestigious Boston publishers J. P. Jewett, also the publisher of *Uncle Tom's Cabin*. We recognize the connection of Leslie's novel to trends popularized by the slave narratives in the alternative title it offers: *Or, Revelations of a Physician's Wife.* Its promise to provide a true eyewitness account plays to the taste for verifiable and "authentic" narratives.[45] Yet her use of a pseudonym for publication calls attention to the degree to which the authenticity of this work is offered as a constructed feature of its overall appeal rather than as a fact of the author's identity. Interestingly, the novel was republished 14 years later in 1869 by another Boston firm, Lee and Shepard.[46] This time—in keeping with the profile of Baker's new publisher—*Cora and the Doctor* was repackaged according to the latest trend in publishing by removing the novel's subtitle. Leslie traded on this appetite for evangelical fiction for the rest of her long and prodigious career as a writer of "Sabbath school books."[47]

There are a host of other writers who, like Leslie, mined the connection to slavery as a means to make it in an emerging and increasingly competitive marketplace. The popularity of the slave narratives provided a compelling reason to develop the material—both nonfiction and fiction—according to the terms of their popularity while also serving the moral purposes so central to abolition. In this connection, we might also look at the career of C. G. Parsons (1807–1864). An ad for his *Inside View of Slavery* appeared alongside ads for other abolitionist works in *The Liberator.* This work, like so many of the others we've considered in this and the earlier chapter, takes advantage of the interest in slavery to sell books. Truth, real-life experience, and a degree of sensationalism were some of the qualities that seemed to most satisfy the reading public interested in the "Startling Disclosures!" of which the advertisement boasts. His book, with a preface written by Harriet Beecher Stowe, claims to be "a four thousandth edition." Though such claims are notoriously unreliable, this particular number puts *An Inside View of Slavery* on par with books by Douglass, Henson, and Brown.

In his introductory note, Parsons—whose byline gives him even greater authority as an eyewitness because he is an M.D.—makes it plain that the book is not only based on facts, but can also lay claim to originality as the research and development of its details were conducted "before any other 'view' of slavery had been published." Parsons claims a place for his work, therefore, by asserting that his is not a work of fashionable fiction but of fact: "Neither its origin nor its preparation has been induced, therefore, by any publication that had preceded it." In other words, the ad's claim is to a greater reader enjoyment and thereby success in the literary marketplace. Like Leslie, Parsons exhibits a degree of market consciousness that demonstrates an awareness of the constructed nature of authorship. What separates Parsons, however, is his claim to truth and authenticity. In a market flooded by works of fiction posing as fact, he distinguishes himself by being frank about the demands of his audience for truth and originality. At the same time, his frankness makes his account more reliable and, therefore, more marketable.

Another author—Nehmiah Adams(1806–1878)—sought to address abolition by writing in both nonfiction and fiction. Adams published numerous religious tracts and sermons, numbering over 20 separate entries. And, like William Wells Brown, Adams collected and arranged music, publishing *Church Pastorals* in 1864 with Ticknor and Fields. His *Southside Views of Slavery* (1854), a work of nonfiction, was based on a three-month visit to the South. It was popular enough to go into a third edition with his original publishers and was then picked up for a fourth edition in 1860 by Ticknor and Fields—publishers of *The Atlantic Monthly* as well as a prestigious list of authors including Hawthorne and Longfellow. In 1861, Adams returned to the literary marketplace with *The Sable Cloud,* an antislavery novel published by Ticknor and Fields. Although he was no stranger to publication, his abolitionist works represent his entrance into high quality publishing through his affiliation with Ticknor and Fields.

In fact, looking at the other Ticknor and Fields titles shows Adams's effort to "cross over" from the abolitionist market to one that was more strictly focused on the evangelical with *Catherine* in a revised edition (1864). In *Catherine,* Adams returns to the genre he had tremendous success with: the literature of consolation. In his *Agnes and a Key to her Coffin. By her father* (1857), we recognize the trace to the slave narratives in the tag, "written by himself." Now transformed to "by her father," this tag emphasizes the tie to personal experience as a significant feature of authorship and textual legitimacy. Arna Bontemps has likened the taste for slave narratives and testimonials to the twentieth-century fascination in Westerns because they "created a parable of the human condition."[48] The adaptation of the market for slave narratives by white writers shows that the genre provided a model for success in a developing literary marketplace.

Another way of understanding the public climate that the popularity of slave narratives promoted is to look at the assortment of publishing venues that took up works with an ideological tie-in to slavery, pro or con. Eager to contribute to the dispute over slavery—and to cash in on the popularity such material was enjoying—authors wrote to satisfy the demand for writing on the subject. Presses great and small strained to produce works that would capitalize on the trend and thus looked for opportunities to publish in this area. An obscure author named William Brisbane would have been completely unknown had he not played to antislavery tastes with his novels *The Fanatic* (1846) and *Amanda* (1848). Both of these novels saw publication through the press at the *American Citizen* office in Philadelphia. A small and very short-lived newspaper, the *American Citizen's* publication of Brisbane's novels most likely represents an effort to produce revenue for the ailing press.

On the other side of the coin, and perhaps more infamously, were writers such as Mary Eastman, author of the reactionary *Aunt Phillis' Cabin.* This 1856 proslavery novel was also published in Philadelphia. But rather than being brought out by a small press associated with one or another aspect of the pro-slavery movement, this novel was published by the commercial house of Lippincott.[49] Interestingly, this title was a departure from the three areas of specialization for the firm. Most of their list was devoted to medicine, religion, and textbooks. The decision to publish Eastman's novel, however, was a lucrative one. The edition I examined at the Boston Public Library indicated that the novel was in its five thousandth printing.[50]

These books by Brisbane and Eastman went through multiple editions, producing income for author and publisher alike. What we must recognize is that the success of their crossover literary productions is a phase of a developing literary marketplace scholars have yet to consider carefully. The fluidity of this marketplace suggests that the literary strategy that made the slave narratives popular was only just becoming an identity—one that would be inextricably tied to race. It would be another ten years before an editor of *The Atlantic Monthly* would assert, in the introduction to "The Freedman's Story" that "none but a negro can fully and correctly depict negro life and character."[51] During the heyday of works such as the ones under examination here, the association of racial identity of the author with representations of slavery had not yet been codified. Thus, writings about slavery—even those tied into the topic ever-so-loosely—sold well in the antebellum literary marketplace.

Yet despite their popularity and success, none of the publications written by white authors includes a portrait of the author as a frontispiece.[52] And though many of these novels did include illustrations, the author was never featured among them. This is universally true of other writers who churned out novel after novel in connection with the battle over slavery. Publishers, it would seem, wanted to promote the idea of truth without venturing a lie. Including an author portrait would have suggested a link between the author and the book's subject matter that was the privilege of autobiography and, in particular, the slave narrative.

Put into print to advance the cause of abolition, slave narratives changed the course of literary history in the United States. At once an important political tool and fresh literary form, their popularity demonstrated—as Stowe's success with *Uncle Tom's Cabin* makes plain—a viable market for the *real.* Looking closely at the popular, but noncanonical, works shows us the thematic use of money as an important indicator of the real. It also makes plain the link between slave narrators and later realists. After all, most of the main proponents of realism wore two hats—one for abolition and one for realism. Even before the generic features popularized by slave narratives became codified by realist texts, they were seized upon by writers and publishers seeking to capitalize on the trend in any way possible. Central, viable, and most of all competitive—these are words I would use to describe African American slave narratives and their impact on the development of American literature.

 3

The Strange Disappearance of Rose Terry Cooke and the Eclipse of American Realism

Slave narratives changed literary tastes in mid-nineteenth-century America. But how can we understand the nature and degree of their impact? The market analysis approach taken in the previous chapter has illuminated the presence of slave narratives as a competitive force in the marketplace. In addition, the discussion of author frontispieces places individual slave narratives within the cultural frame of authorship. Now I'd like to focus on how the slave narratives shaped literary history by considering their impact on one popular author, Rose Terry Cooke. Her career was fueled by the forces of abolition and the growth of print media. Her writings will help us address the question: How might slave narratives have influenced Rose Terry Cooke?

Although few today read her work, Rose Terry Cooke (1827–1892) once held a prominent place among the short-fiction writers known as local colorists. Her career began before the Civil War and she gained wide notice when her work was featured in the inaugural issue of *The Atlantic Monthly* in 1857.[1] Many of Cooke's stories utilize the vocabulary of slavery and thus exhibit important aspects of Cooke's adaptation of abolitionist issues to other humanitarian subjects. Her stories were written during the period African Americanists refer to as the "golden age of the slave narrative" because of the form's ascendancy; this period is also referred to by literary critics Susan Belasco Smith and Kenneth Price as "the golden age of periodicals," and many of the magazines in which Cooke's work appears also published slave narratives and their reviews.[2]

Cooke's work reveals a confluence of forces—biographical and historical, economic and literary, generic and ideological.[3] My discussion of these forces and their relevance to the larger question at stake in this chapter will help me challenge received notions about the sources of realism. In looking carefully at one writer's efforts both to profit from publication and to reform readers, we gain insight into the ways that literary history streamlines messy ideological engagements by regulating discursive patterns through canon formation. Examining Cooke's popularity, fictional works, and publishing venues will restore the rockiness of the terrain out of which realism grew. To begin, I'd like to explore Cooke's popularity as a writer.

First and foremost, Rose Terry Cooke was a popular writer. She made her living by the pen. Yet, despite her popularity, there is only one known contemporary source on Cooke's life. Written by Harriet Prescott Spofford, this portrait was included in *Our Famous Women* (1884).[4] Cooke was featured along with other such luminaries as Louisa May Alcott, Susan B. Anthony, Clara Barton, Lydia Maria Child, Margaret Fuller, Julia Ward Howe, Lucy Larcom, and Harriet Beecher Stowe. According to Spofford's account, Cooke descended from the blue-blooded Calvinists many of her stories would later mock, and thus started life with all the advantages of a New Englander. Born in Hartford, Connecticut on February 17, 1827 to Anne Wright Harlbut and Henry Wadsworth Terry, her family was well to do. Her paternal grandfather was a president of the Hartford Bank and a member of Congress, and her maternal grandfather was a shipmaster who sailed around the world. By the time Rose Terry Cooke was sixteen years old, however, the family fortune had diminished. Like Louisa May Alcott, several years her junior, she always felt the pressure to contribute to the economic well being of her household. After taking up teaching for several years, Cooke returned home to Hartford and began her literary career.[5]

Primarily a magazinist, Cooke published poetry, short fiction, two novels, and essays. [6] Her popularity can be measured in the number and variety of publishing outlets she relied on; it can also be noted in the peculiar fact that Cooke was frequently the subject of attempts at impersonation.[7] Readers enjoyed her fiction, poetry, and essays in the pages of secular publications such as *Graham's Magazine, Putnam's, Harper's* and *The Atlantic Monthly,* as well as evangelical outlets that included *The Independent, The Congregationalist,* and *The Christian Union,* popular Protestant publications. According to Price and Smith, "the periodical—far more than the book—was a *social* text, involving complex relationships among writers, readers, editors, publishers, printers, and distributors."[8] Through its editorial practices, the magazine industry encouraged this sort of dialogue between readers and writers as a basis for reader interest and Rose Terry Cooke's writing developed in response to and in conjunction with this social context. Thus, tracing Cooke's interactions with and contributions to the literary marketplace will help us better understand the impetus for the emerging taste for realism.

Some writers might find publishing in so many different places inhibiting, but Cooke's stories show that the wide range of publishing venues encouraged an assortment of narrative strategies customized to each one. Uniting the topical issues of abolition with the ethical concerns of humanitarianism, Cooke reshaped reader expectations. The wide range of publication venues suggests that she crafted a relationship with a diverse swath of readers and in so doing, intervened in the construction of literary tastes. Indeed, a close look at Cooke's rhetorical strategies—the rhetoric of abolition and its use of the humanitarian narrative—reveals greater resistance to the national political economy underwritten by canonized local colorists. Today we read slave narratives for their aesthetic value rather than as a means to abolish slavery, but Cooke's writing has yet to be appreciated beyond its didacticism. The eclipse of Rose Terry Cooke's literary reputation has much to do with her work's commitment to reform and exposes a more important cover-up in American literary history: the erasure of slave narratives as a source for the development of realism in the United States.

I. Rose Terry Cooke and the Literary Marketplace

In 1857, Cooke's career was established enough for her work to be featured in what was to become one of the premier magazines, *The Atlantic Monthly.* Its editor, the poet and essayist, James Russell Lowell (1819–1891) announced the magazine's priorities on the masthead: "A Magazine of Literature, Art, and Politics."[9] Rose Terry (Cooke)'s short story, "Sally Parson's Duty," appeared in this inaugural issue.

The Atlantic Monthly sought to establish links between literature, art, and politics. The magazine's layout encouraged readers to think about these connections. Like the nineteenth-century reader, the magazine did not separate genres—poetry from fiction, fiction from news—but rather intermingled various forms of writing by eliminating the distinction between them in the physical arrangement of the magazine. For instance, "Sally Parson's Duty" was preceded by Longfellow's poem, "Santa Filomena," and followed by an article written by Harvard professor Charles Eliot Norton describing an extensive art exhibit on view in Manchester, England. And without a table of contents, the magazine plainly invited readers to peruse its pages as one would a book—from start to finish.

One of the only publishing houses of the mid-nineteenth century to survive in any form, Ticknor and Fields, the publishing company of *The Atlantic Monthly,* was able to do so through its marketing savvy.[10] Their famous "blue and gold" editions opened up a new market for American literature, in part creating "classic" American works through an attractive binding. At the same time, they also figured prominently as publishers of works connected with abolition. Their strategy to create, maintain, and develop a market niche ran through all that they did. As Michael Winship explains, "in the mid-nineteenth century Ticknor and Fields was able to select for publication texts that appealed to the literary culture at the time, and further, to arrange to have these packaged and distributed as books in ways that encouraged their acceptance as works of literary merit."[11] An author's literary reputation was a direct product of where he or she published, and an affiliation with a prestigious press such as this one was the mark of a successful writer of the time.[12] During the course of Cooke's career, Ticknor and Fields brought out one collection of poems, two short story collections, and two novels—five of the nine books Cooke had published in her lifetime.[13]

Cooke also benefited from Ticknor and Fields's business conduct. Among its practices, Ticknor and Fields cultivated relationships with its authors.[14] Letters reveal how involved authors could be in the publication process, even if authors did not always call the shots. It was in part this practice that made Ticknor and Fields so successful. Consulting over a collection of her poetry they would soon be publishing, Cooke advised Ticknor and Fields that she "can tell which [poems] have been most popular, and should be guided by that" in making the selection.[15] She had confidence in her ability to make the selection and, despite the common practice of dictating the contents of their books, Ticknor and Fields uncharacteristically abided by her choices.[16]

In the case of the collection of poems, she makes it plain that her expectations for the volume are small, opting for 10 percent royalties after the first thousand copies are sold rather than risk financing the printing costs herself (as Sojourner Truth had). She explains her decision with characteristic clear-sightedness: "I never have looked forward to this publication as anything but a stepping-stone."[17] Mindful of those who have also served as stepping stones in her career as a writer, she closes the letter with a request that the volume be dedicated to Charles Dana, the editor at the *New York Tribune* who first gave her poems a venue.

But it is to James Fields's recognition of market trends that she really owes her professional standing. Largely self-educated, James Fields apprenticed as a bookseller at the Old Corner Bookstore in Boston. It is fabled that Fields's market sense was so canny that, while working there "he gained a reputation among his fellows for being able to predict not only what books would sell but even what book each customer entering the store would buy."[18] His work at the bookstore, coupled with his love of literature, sharpened his sense of "literature as a commodity."[19] His career is proof that "the mid-nineteenth-century Boston cultural elite was far less a hereditary class than a meritocracy with diverse roots of access."[20] In his capacity as editor and publisher, Fields implemented practices that encouraged literary production as a business and thus kept the field open relying on the democracy of the marketplace. To further promote his authors, Fields introduced a semiannual index of contributors—names of authors had formerly been withheld—in 1862. By 1870 *The Atlantic Monthly* published everything except reviews with author by-lines.[21] And it was Fields who urged Cooke to publish under her own name rather than the pseudonym "A. W. H." (her mother's initials) she had been using. This new practice was part and parcel of Fields's efforts to make authorship in America a lucrative business. Thus, Fields joins Garrison among the ranks of successful entrepreneurs of the print world.

As for *The Atlantic Monthly*'s connections to abolition, it was the only literary publication to subscribe to *The Liberator.* According to the subscription lists, *The Atlantic Monthly* held not just one, but three subscriptions.[22] Not surprisingly, Cooke's publishers were closely allied with abolitionists in the Boston area and came to represent the New England culture machine. Longfellow, Lowell, Whittier, and Stowe were among the authors whose works were published in *The Atlantic Monthly* and by Ticknor and Fields. And once William Lloyd Garrison shut down *The Liberator* in 1865, his youngest son Frances Jackson Garrison joined the editorial staff of Houghton Mifflin, the publishing company that Ticknor and Fields later became.[23] At the same time, another of Garrison's sons, Wendell Phillips Garrison, became the literary editor of the *Nation.* He held the post until 1906.

Magazine editors and publishers sought topical connections to contemporary issues in order to tap the liberal capitalism that ran throughout the reform-minded readership. Like many other writers working in the Northeast, Cooke was caught up in abolition, the political struggle of her day, and her literary works retain those marks.[24] Clearly the ties between abolition and the developing publishing industry ran deep. A close reading of two of the short stories Cooke published in *The Atlantic Monthly* show just how deep by helping us understand how Cooke developed the humanitarian impulse of the slave narratives into what I am calling humanitarian realism.

II. From Humanitarian Narrative to Humanitarian Realism: "Sally Parson's Duty" and "The Ring Fetter"

"Sally Parson's Duty" and "The Ring Fetter" appeared in *The Atlantic Monthly* in 1857 and 1859 respectively.[25] In both stories Cooke carefully weaves her critique of gender norms with her rejection of the narrative practices she associates with sentimentalism. She saw sentimentalism as often transforming real suffering and social injustice simply into a vehicle for the reader's experience of pathos. Often using the direct address mode in her stories, Cooke renegotiated her contract with readers over precisely these issues. In her efforts to readjust the terms of reader engagement, Cooke introduced key qualities of what I am calling humanitarian realism. The use of the generic standards popularized by the slave narratives such as authenticating details, dialect, and a frank treatment of the body turn these stories about marriage into a critique of the institution itself and the sentimental fiction that she sees as romanticizing it.

Readers of "Sally Parson's Duty" find out, along with Sally, what she can do to express her political views on the American Revolution. Sailor Long Snapps, an old seaman who has become a permanent resident of the Parson household, assures her that she has considerable power; should she decide to stand by her politics she will be able to "twist young fellers round, an' make 'em sail under the right colors."[26] Effecting a Yankee *Lysistrata,* Sally refuses to marry George Tucker, the man she loves, because he is "a Britisher and a Tory."[27] Evoking an image of slavery implicitly drawn from the Declaration of Independence, Sally proclaims, "I can't stand by cool and see men driven like dumb beasts by another man, if he got a crown, and never be let to speak for themselves."[28] Calling to mind the treatment of slaves as human chattel forced to serve at another's will for another's gain, Cooke excites reader sympathy. Caught up in her humanitarian concerns, readers delight when Sally holds out for her ideal, and wins. Due to the pressure Sally exerts, George Tucker ends up on the Yankee side. Injured by the Tories in the first battle of the Revolution, we leave Sally at his side happily nursing him.

The plot of "Sally Parson's Duty" uses the spirit of the American Revolution to provide a basis for its main conflict, drawing on the tension of the impending Civil War. Its opening lines establish a link between revolutionary times and the local present using authenticating details to call forth an image of the land: "The sun that shines on eastern Massachusetts, specially on buttercups and dandelions, and providentially on potatoes, looks down on no greener fields in these days then it saw in the spring of 1775."[29] And though Sally Parson's first words "Dear me! a real war comin!" pertain to the revolutionary war, her exclamation invites readers to think of the imminent conflict between North and South.

The question that the end of the story poses, however, harkens the reader back to its title. Sally Parson reasoned that it was her "duty" as a woman during wartime to use her only possession—herself—as a tool to defeat the Tories. When asked if she would have helped George had he not switched over to the Yankee side, the old sailor responds for her: "'I 'xpect she'd 'a' done her dooty,' said Long Snapps dryly; and Sally laughed."[30] Her laughter leaves the reader to wonder what exactly that duty is.

The fact that *The Atlantic Monthly* selected this story for its premier issue guides us toward a message that would have been sanctioned by the magazine. Sally's story must have spoken to issues that editors at *The Atlantic Monthly* had identified as constitutive of the nineteenth-century New England readership they were targeting. Thus the lesson her experience teaches—that the personal is political—is a message consonant with the public-spirited views *The Atlantic Monthly* is promoting. But what of the story's literary merit?

In addition to the message that women have the ability to shape the political choices of the men who care about them, the story also offers a referendum on the popular use of dialect. A form of speech most directly associated with the depiction of blacks in slave narratives and minstrelsy, Cooke renders her characters' speech in the same idiom. Resembling the "childlike gibberish" spoken by popular culture's representations of blacks, Cooke's characters are posited as aboriginal and primitive through the use of dialect.[31] Speaking in dialect held significant social stigma. As Jean Baker observes about dialect, "the effect, in a society that increasingly associated language with nationhood, was to widen the chasm between a responsible white citizenry and a feckless black population unable to pronounce even the words of freedom." In the case of Cooke's white characters, however, dialect lends them a degree of realism that would otherwise be lacking. Long Snapp's declaration, "'tis a kinder pity you a'n't a man, Sally; mebbe you'd argufy him round then," suggests a homespun wisdom rather than the worldly ignorance then associated with dialect in the mouths of black speakers. To readers accustomed to dialect as a means to degrade characters, Cooke's use must have compelled them to reimagine the generic uses of dialect and the politics these uses implied.

But perhaps even more surprising is Cooke's acknowledgement of the bodily pleasure marriage might bring in "Sally Parson's Duty." Gently introducing the materiality of the body by euphemism and allusion, Cooke suggests pleasure as a motivating principle for marriage. Midway through the story, Long Snapps breaks out with another one of his salty observations: "Ye never see a woman 't didn't get married for dooty yet" he exclaims, "there ar'n't nary one on 'em darst to say they wanted ter."[32] To be sure that readers catch the full meaning of Long Snapps's assertion, Cooke uses Sally's exclamation of "Oh! Mr. Long!" to move the conversation forward. "Well, Sally, it's nigh about so" he ruminates. "You han't lived a hundred year. Some o' these days you'll know your dooty."[33] Judging by the reaction that Sally—who blushes—and the three young men present—who "snigger"—readers must conclude that "dooty" here is the physical pleasures of marriage rather than the moral ones.

Moving into direct address with "Forgive the word ["snigger"], gentle and fair readers," Cooke continues to rework reader sensibility by poking fun at literary coyness. Addressing reading practices and tastes ruling literary decorum, Cooke urges: "it means what I mean and no other word expresses it; let us be graphic and die!"[34] By parodying the spirit of William Lloyd Garrison's admonition to be "as harsh as truth," Cooke makes her own case for rejecting literary propriety as falsely pretty and potentially dangerous. The lack of frank and direct language might allow readers to be seduced by the romance of fiction and to fail to act politically. As with so many of her stories, Cooke relies on a reader's intelligence as a means to establish identification with readers and thus initiate reform.

Readers of these stories will be as struck with Cooke's radical ideas about marriage as by the story's links with the rhetorical strategies of the slave narratives. As legal theorist Elizabeth Clark has observed, the fundamental trope of the suffering slave produced by evangelical abolitionism became "incorporated as a persistent strand in our rights tradition."[35] Rose Terry Cooke's "The Ring Fetter" replaces the image of the suffering slave with the suffering wife, the story's protagonist.

"The Ring Fetter" undermines the pleasure readers find in the marriage plot by creating impossible romances within the larger story proper. The first "romance" is between the father and mother. Cooke uses North and South sectional differences to show the marriage's destiny through the lineage of the two characters. Her mother was a Baltimore beauty whose Southern frailties could not survive the birth of her daughter while her father represents the Northern ideal of the educated professional: a judge. Thus, her lineage brings together North and South, though the story's outcome predicts an unhappy union. A lively and precocious girl, Mehitable (Hitty) was sturdy yet strangely ephemeral because of her "mixed blood."

The next "romance" is the suggested incest between father and daughter that begins when Mr. Hyde realizes that he has a "pretty daughter," one that he later insists on possessing.[36] She wastes her youth nursing him through his terminal illness: "But now Judge Hyde was dead; nineteen years of petulant, helpless, hopeless wretchedness were at last over, and all that his daughter cared to live for was gone; she was an orphan, without near relatives, without friends, old, and tired out."[37] With her father gone, she marries and thus becomes the victim of a marriage plot that does her in.

Like so many of the protagonists of the later realists, such as Edith Wharton's Lily Bart and Henry James's Isabel Archer, Hitty's problems are set in motion by money. Upon her father's death, she inherited $50,000.

The prospect of this sum attracts Abner Dimock to woo her. The story tells how Hitty, in the third and truly impossible romance, is bound as wife/slave by the "ring fetter" to husband/owner, Abner Dimock. She is the tormented victim of an avaricious fiend to whom she is "chained for life" or, until death, while the ring fetter binds her finger. The economic independence afforded to her by her father's estate ceases to be in her control as she enters wedlock.

Referring to the married state as a "double life," this story presses the case against marriage as the defining role of a woman's life.[38] "Neither law nor novelists altogether displace this same persistent fact," Cooke writes, "and a woman lives, in all capacities of suffering and happiness, not only her wonted, but a double life, when legally and religiously she binds herself with bond and vow to another soul."[39] Cooke's assertion that the married woman leads a double life is in direct opposition to the kind of gender fulfillment and personal reconciliation marriage was supposed to yield women. Though Hitty expects happiness from romance and marriage, her experience runs counter to those wishes in every way: "Happy would it have been for Hitty Hyde," the narrative notes with sarcasm, "if the legal fiction [of matrimonial bliss] had chimed the actual existent fact!"[40] Cooke uses Hitty's circumstances to illuminate the systematic loss of autonomy dictated by the social norms of white womanhood. Hitty's former free state and relations included control over her inheritance; her present bondage to Abner places such power in abeyance. It is a strange example of supply and demand that emphasizes, not intrinsic virtues as the domestic novel and sentimental philosophy would have it, but the transferable material value linked with literary realism and capitalism.

Cooke likens marriage to a slave economy positing the husband Abner Dimock as an analogy for the slave master. He cruelly torments his wife Hitty, valuing her only for her productive/reproductive capabilities:

> It is true that if she had died then [after the birth of their son], Abner Dimock would have regretted her death; for by certain provisions of her father's will, in case of death, the real estate, otherwise at her own disposal, became a trust for her child or children, and such contingency ill suited Mr. Dimock's plans. So long as Hitty held a rood of land or a coin of silver at her disposal, it was also at his; but trustees are not women, happily for the world at large, and the contemplation of that fact brought Hitty Hyde's husband into a state of mind well fitted to give him real joy at her recovery.[41]

I have quoted this passage at length in order to trace Abner Dimock's metamorphosis from an individual to a stereotype. Reference to "Abner Dimock" (in the first line of the quotation) becomes the more reserved and formal "Mr. Dimock" (1. 4–5) and then settles on "Hitty Hyde's husband" (1. 7–8). This movement from given and family name to the descriptive title sketches the trajectory of their marital relationship. The use of Hitty's "maiden" name of Hyde underscores the fact that their marriage is no union.

This passage also shows how Hitty's experience with motherhood in "The Ring Fetter" brings her peril home to the reader. Hitty is neither a woman nor a mother in her husband's eyes. She is simply a financial resource to be depleted. Frequently, Dimock muses about life without Hitty, but these fantasies always end with the realization that at her demise the money also ends. Rather than seeing the birth of their child as a gateway to future generations, Dimock views the baby as another claim on Hitty's fortune.

Cooke sketches other similarities between marriage and slave status. In thinking of Hitty's relationship to himself, Abner realizes that he has been made master through marriage: "She could not leave him; she was utterly in his power; she was his,—like his boots, his gun, his dog; and till he should tire of her and fling her into some lonely chamber to waste and die, she was bound to serve him."[42] As a theme, Cooke uses the transformation of Hitty from a free and independent woman to a captive held as chattel to suggest a link to slave status. Just as the slave owner maintained (and sometimes preferred) his own mulatto offspring, he was also preserving (and promoting) their market value. Likewise, Hitty Dimock is maintained for her productive power as potential capital.

In this story, the law and operation of the legal system is found to be systematically faulty. Cooke includes a passage from Blackstone on dowry rights to capture the one-sided nature of the law on this subject: "the law is so tender of a woman that it takes care of her," the story notes ironically. Yet, Mr. Hyde's will can only protect and provide for her as long as she stays unmarried, a perpetual daughter. In the event of Hitty's marriage, the inheritance will be controlled by her husband. Though the will is meant to protect Hitty by compensating her spouse as long as he takes care of her, it also defines the terms of Hitty's torment: her fortune is his as long as she lives so that the preservation of her life is the prolongation of his income. Abner Dimock can only have what is immediately present as long as Hitty lives; upon her death her body and her fortune will cease to be for him. Hitty's legacy, bequeathed to her through a patrimonial inheritance is then handed down to her children directly. Thus, Hitty's estate circumvents traditional patrimony, ironically like the laws that ruled that children of slave women follow the condition of their mother.

Hitty's relation to the child offers a striking contrast to her husband's views. Hitty sees in her child, still a clumsy toddler, sprawled out on the grass, the hope of future comforts. The narrator muses,

> Perhaps the budding blossom of promise might become floral and fruitful; perhaps her child might yet atone for the agony of the past;—a time might come when she should sit in that door, white-haired and trembling with age, but as peaceful as the autumn day, watching the sports of his children, while his strong arm sustained her into the valley of shadow, and his tender eyes lit the way.[43]

Her hopes outline the new order; she is focused on the comfort offered by future generations. Interestingly, her father-in-law intrudes upon this idyllic scene and interrupts her reverie. The shadow of her son's progenitor falls doubly upon him. Described as "a strange, tottering old figure," the grandfather is not only decrepit, "his whole air [is] squalid, hopeless and degraded."[44] The trace of a register of a nineteenth-century racial paradigm is here, signified by "degraded." But the use of this paradigm departs from the usual practice of white female writers of this era. Cooke invokes race not to glorify Anglo-Saxon ancestry, but to mock it through critique—a harbinger of Cooke's developing anti-New Englandism. The child recognizes his own fate in his grandfather and "met his advances with an ominous scream."[45] The little boy intuitively links the patriarchal influence in his life with harm. He is prescient: the boy will shortly be killed at the hands of his father.

The reason for the grandfather's visit—to warn his son—compels the Dimocks, along with Abner's partner in crime, Ben, to bolt. Though the crime he has committed remains unnamed thus far, Cooke figures him as the counterfeiter he is in the scene that follows. As the family flees their home and the law, the child, frightened, cold, and hungry, cries loudly. Abner Dimock "turned round on his seat with an oath, snatched the child from its mother's arms, and rolled it closely in a blanket."[46] In a parody of the image of a happy family, Abner Dimock "grasped his wife tightly with one arm, and with the other" holding their son for a chilling moment, then "dropped the child into the street."[47] Readers would immediately recognize the psychological landscape as the same traversed by Stowe's Eliza when she risked drowning in the freezing Ohio river rather than undergo separation from her child. We witness Hitty's suffering: "her child fell, Hitty shrieked with such a cry as only the heart of a mother could send out over a newly-murdered infant. Shriek on shriek, fast and loud and long, broke the slumbers of the village."[48] Without a doubt, the trauma that destroys Hitty's will to survive is the murder of her child. Her suicide also draws on Stowe's Eliza, for when Hitty leaps into the river to her death, she destroys herself as property. Hitty's suicide makes clear the meaning of the story's subtitle, "A New England Tragedy." Her tragic loss is not merely her life but the independence she was robbed of through marriage.

Cooke's stylistic choices here and elsewhere encourage a sense that the events depicted are "real," immune to the conventions of romance. For despite sentimentalism's use of homespun and quotidian settings, real issues (such as slavery) were often translated into white middle-class evangelical ideology.[49] At around the same time as Cooke was publishing, Harriet Jacobs expressed a similar reservation about sentimentalism. When Jacobs's text was being circulated, Harriet Beecher Stowe suggested that she incorporate Jacobs's story into her *Key to Uncle Tom's Cabin.* Jacobs responded angrily that her story "needed no romance" to validate the experiences retold in it.[50] In order to articulate this new emphasis on the bodily, Cooke turned to narrative strategies literary historians associate with slave narratives, forming a literary style we can call humanitarian realism for its social aims.

III. Cooke's Use of Physical Suffering: Are Black and Blue Local Colors?

Cooke chose not to reprint "The Ring Fetter" in any of her published collections. Yet, she returned to the marriage plot in two stories that mark important stages in her career: "Mrs. Flint's Married Experience" and "How Celia Changed Her Mind." After publishing over a hundred stories, Cooke's confidence in her literary reputation showed when she chided William Dean Howells for his refusal to publish "Mrs. Flint's Married Experience" in *The Atlantic Monthly.* Cooke wrote with a smirk, "aren't you a little bit sorry to think you did not take [the story] when you see it turned out with Abbey's illustrations in such good shape"[51]

Cooke's placement of "Mrs. Flint's Married Experience" in *Harper's* signals an important stage in her career as a successful writer. The story was featured in the December 1880 publication of *Harper's*—the one editors paid special attention to, for with it also came a renewal notice. This issue was typically well illustrated and included material best suited for attracting subscriptions. Also printed in the issue in which Cooke's story appeared is the first installment of Constance Fenimore Woolson's *Anne* and a later installment of James's *Washington Square.* Immediately preceding Cooke's tale is Sarah Orne Jewett's "Two Mornings," a short poem that explores the impact of class on the experience of grief by taking the point of view of two different people—a lady and a page. The lady must grieve in public while the page may remove himself from view to experience his sorrow in private. Cooke's story is lavishly illustrated—more so than the other pieces in the issue. It contains four woodcuts even though the story only takes up a little over 22 pages. As it draws to a conclusion, the copy flows into the next article, "Recent Movements in Woman's Education"—an article that describes and encourages women's education in the United States and abroad. The message that this issue of *Harper's* most strongly imparts is that a focus on the lives of women and women's issues is market-wise.

In this story, Cooke's return to the marriage plot is marked by an important biographical event: her own marriage late in life. Some critics have even speculated that it is her experience that gives these stories their bitter edge.[52] Cooke's short story, "Mrs. Flint's Married Experience," details the abusive ideology under which her character suffers. The initial method of domination is economic—although it becomes clear that the result of this kind of domination cannot be fathomed merely in monetary terms. Part of what makes this story interesting is the fact that its central character gives up her respectable identity as the "Widow Gold" to take on the culturally less-exalted role of "Mrs. Flint" even though she has the rare privilege, as the Widow Gold, of financial independence. Her marriage legally strips her of her inheritance; she is left utterly dependent on the whims of her husband for her "living."

The marriage, needless in terms of social status and security, signifies the presence of deeper structures of domination than mere economic ones. Cooke's perceptive eye notes the intricacy of victimization. Silenced within and without the household by her own beliefs, Mrs. Flint cannot even voice her suffering to her daughter without blaspheming against her God and Calvinist doctrines of free will.[53] In the mother/daughter relationship Cooke depicts, she inserts another impossible romance, that of mother and daughter. The vocabulary used to describe their relationship is sentimental and Mrs. Gold assumes the role of the jilted lover when she accepts Mr. Flint's proposal. Believing "her girl was no longer hers," Mrs. Gold abandons the safety and comfort of her widowhood to become a wife once more.[54]

Throughout the story, Cooke carefully distinguishes the capacity to suffer from the sordid scene of suffering itself, a strategy typical of the slave narratives. To that end, she indicts secular culture with the same vigor she uses against the religious mechanisms that contain Mrs. Flint in her marriage. Mr. Flint, whose Christian name "Amassa" sounds like "a master," is given qualities similar to the slave master, a figure who often sought to reconcile the secular aim of making a living with the spiritual charge to lead the children of Ham. Mr. Flint, a prominent member of the church, teaches his wife the same lesson that Frederick Douglass observed: "The cowskin makes as deep a gash in my flesh, when wielded by a professed saint, as it does when wielded by an open sinner." Clearly, religion is no guarantee for humanitarian actions. In fact, Mrs. Flint's attempt to expose the cruelty of her husband is silenced by the clergy on the same basis that a slave's complaint of ill-treatment would be and had been silenced according to Douglass and others. "Speak not evil of dignities," the local parson adjures, "Amassy Flint is a deacon of Bassett church. It does not become you to revile him."[55] As a wife, Mrs. Flint loses her right to appeal to the church for justice to her person despite the ill-treatment she has received from her husband. Protected by his racial, gender, and social status, Mr. Flint is free to abuse his wife, even unto death.

Slavery here is more than a trope for marriage. Cooke's argument against marriage goes beyond a simple analogy with slavery by enmeshing itself in contemporary politics. By naming the doctor who comes to save Mrs. Flint "Grant" after the general of the Civil War and the country's eighteenth president who was on death's doorstep in 1880 when this story was published, Cooke seems to be holding out hope for the reconstruction of marriage as an institution as she and others hoped for a successfully reconstructed South. According to Jean Edward Smith's recent biography, Grant's presidential record has been overshadowed by his Civil War deeds. Known in his own time for reimplementing programs to ensure and enforce civil rights for African Americans after Andrew Jackson left office, Grant served eight years and thus had a remarkable mandate from the people.[56] Marred by systematic corruption both in the story and in history, however, reconstruction failed. Using this history as a backdrop for her story, we witness the tragic results of reconstruction's failure. Declining to follow Dr. Grant's instructions, Mrs. Flint dies. Thus the story braids together two scenarios, one marital and the other political. Yet, all is not lost.

Though Mrs. Flint is the central character, there are several alternative readings of the marital experience in this story. Through the minor figure of Mrs. Flint's niece Mabel, Cooke offers a radical agenda of empowerment instead of the tacit acknowledgement of the degeneration of New England culture. Rather than leave her female characters in the home, to be battered still again, Cooke stimulates the next generation to look beyond, and more importantly, to overcome the structures confining them. Mabel functions within the frame of the story as a kind of double, suggesting patterns for living beyond those already in existence. The fact that Mabel's courtship takes place at "the little gate"[57] outside Mrs. Flint's house—instead of in "the keepin' room"[58] where Mrs. Flint's prenuptial negotiations took place—is just one of the suggestive details woven into the story. Mabel's romance is free from the limits of domesticity that confine Mrs. Flint's.

Once Mabel becomes the custodian of the abused Mrs. Flint, we understand the full force of Mabel's advantage. In the end, she is both to witness and judge of Mrs. Flint's suffering. Mabel's question, "Haven't you got the right to save your life?"[59] is answered directly by Mrs. Flint's death. Her death solidifies Mabel's sense that the systematic oppression of her aunt had religious, cultural, and physical origins. Rejoining Mr. Flint's pious claims,

Mabel anticipates Huck Finn's wish to go to hell rather than give Jim up with "If you're pious, I hope I shall be a reprobate."[60] The story ends on a sober note—one sounded in Cooke's "Miss Lucinda" published thirty years earlier—with a reference to a resurrection parable in which Jesus shows that even though a woman is widowed and married by seven brothers, she will be no one's wife in heaven. Notwithstanding Mrs. Flint's first and happier marriage to Mr. Gold, heaven is, in Cooke's estimation, being a single woman.

"How Celia Changed Her Mind," published in what would be her last collection, continues the theme developed by the figures of Mrs. Flint's daughter Mindwell and more radical niece Mabel. As far as one can tell, Cooke did not seek magazine publication for this story, which indicates that she didn't think its message would be popular enough for the literary marketplace.[61] Since we know that she took care to tailor work for particular venues, it's not surprising that she choose to smuggle this story into a collection; this format would grant her more freedom than having to submit to the close scrutiny of a magazine editor. And, as we saw in her earlier collection of poetry, her choices for inclusion held sway with Ticknor and Fields. Upon close reading of the story, this hypothesis gains additional credibility.

In "How Celia Changed Her Mind," the protagonist, Celia, is an old maid who condemns her status as such until she has the opportunity to learn how lucky she had been independent and self-sufficient. She arranges her own marriage and helps another woman in the story marry. But she regrets her actions when both marriages end in disaster. The story concludes with Celia as a widow, adopting the children of the friend she had helped to the altar (now deceased). In this act, she assumes all of the most exalted roles: friend, mother, and widow. She has learned her way around the ideology, the economy, and the law. Celia has overcome her old social injunctions against spinsterhood. And she has gotten the better of her legal relationship to her dead husband. Despite the fact that he disinherited her, she still manages to get her "thirds"—the portion of the estate a legal spouse is entitled to—as well as the benefit of a life insurance policy he overlooked. And, when asked about her inheritance, Celia quickly responds, "I earned it."

Celia's inheritance becomes a symbol of her mastery in the story. And like the slave narrators with whom Cooke shares the literary marketplace, this author uses money as an index for her character's progress. As Celia heads a Thanksgiving dinner for a group of her old-maid friends she declares:

> I've got means, and, as I've said before, I earned 'em. I don't feel noway obliged to him for 'em; he didn't mean it. But now I can I'm goin' to adopt

> Rosy Barker's two children, and fetch em' up to be dyed-in-the-wool old maids; and every year, so long as I live, I'm goin' to keep an old maids' Thanksgivin' for a kind of burnt-offering, sech as the Bible tells about, for I've changed my mind clear down to the bottom, and as I go the hull figure with the 'postle Paul when he speaks about the onmarried, 'It is better if she so abide.' Now let's go to work at the victuals. [62]

This is a woman who not only owns herself free and clear, but who is also in a position to invest in the future through her adoption of Rosy Barker's children.

The future that Celia imagines here, though, is noticeably free of men. Her revisions on the traditional family structure alone suggest a radical departure from the system of which she is a product. Through the adoption of Rosy Barker's children, Celia once again uses the legal system to her advantage. As Michael Grossberg points out, adoption provides "a legal mechanism for completely severing the bonds of birth" and in this case, Celia's wish to sever the bonds to patriarchal culture steadies her aim.[63] Her wish to raise these two little girls to be "dyed-in-the-wool old maids" is a wish to undo the patriarchal structures that have confined her. Gone from this situation is a marriage and with it the heterosexual romance tradition that has set the stage for young girls and women to sell their birthright for a mess of pottage, or what Cooke calls "the freemasonry of married women."[64] Celia soon discovers "how few among them were more than household drudges, the servants of their families, worked to the verge of exhaustion, and neither thanked nor rewarded for their pains."[65]

Despite all of her allusions to slavery, readers had to wait for "A Hard Lesson," published in *The Continent* in June of 1884, for Cooke's explicit views on race. The story of a Southern plantation farmer and owner of many slaves, "A Hard Lesson" introduces its main character in his sick bed, attended to by his half brother and slave, Stephen. Louis Fontaine, known as "Judge" Fontaine, is suffering from an unknown illness that does not respond to treatment. He is advised to leave his family and journey North to take the cure in Saratoga and to consult with learned medical men in New York. Initially, several black spots are the only visible signs of illness on the Judge's body.

The Judge travels North. As he travels he begins to regain his health, but the spots spread in direct proportion to recovery. Once he has completely recuperated, the Judge has also become "black." Anticipating themes that Twain would later handle in his 1894 *Pudd'n Head Wilson,* the irony of the story intensifies: "Louis Fontaine was a negro to every eye but his own."[66] What follows is a reversal of the fugitive slave experience. As Louis Fontaine attempts to return to his Southern plantation, Stephen, his half brother and slave, abandons him for freedom in Canada.

The story expresses a radically progressive attitude toward conceptions of race by representing race as mutable and even accidental. Cooke uses Judge Fontaine's racial reversal of fortune to uncover assumptions about the natural status of race. Judge Fontaine finds out what life is like on the other side of the color line. Yet, despite his many experiences of disenfranchisement—he is denied his seat on the train, a room in the hotel where he was often a guest, and he fears being caught after dark without a pass—he never abandons his view of race as a natural signifier. Rather, his experiences spur him on to further refine his prejudices by reassuring himself that since he was not born black, he cannot be black. Shaken when his wife is unable to accept him, he finds comfort once his dog recognizes him for who he "really" is. Louis observes, "the dog knows me, but not you—" and leaves his sentence unfinished as he notices that Mrs. Fontaine "trembled from head to foot; every inborn prejudice of race and usage revolted at the assertion that this *black* was her *husband*."[67] The narrative registers his loss grammatically: Judge Fontaine loses his status as a noun (husband), he is now only the adjective used as a noun to designate the slave population (black).

What kinds of conclusions can we draw from a story such as this one? We might be tempted to lump Cooke's work in with other literary productions from the pens of fervent abolitionists—writers of her day, such as Harriet Beecher Stowe and John Greenleaf Whittier. Indeed, her abolitionist commitment has been memorialized in a painting by Eastman Johnson (see figure 3.1).

Called *The Freedom Ring,* this image commemorates Cooke's gift of an opal ring as the only means she had available to help ransom a young girl out of slavery. Christened "Rose Ward," after Rose Terry and Henry Ward Beecher (in whose church she was made free), she was ever after known as "Little Pinky." A writer for the antislavery *Independent* declared, "The scene is likely never to be forgotten by those who witnessed it."[68] In 1927, Rose Ward (Mrs. James Hunt) returned the ring to Plymouth Church, where it is now on view.[69] But even without the ring or the painting, there is much more powerful evidence of Cooke's commitment to abolition in her work.

With rhetorical and thematic connections to slavery, titles such as "The Ring Fetter" and "Our Slave" keep Cooke's commitment active by drawing on the discursive practices popular among early abolitionists of the mid-nineteenth-century Woman's Movement.[70] Stories such as "The Ring Fetter" and "Mrs. Flint's Married Experience" detail the connections between Cooke's conception of womanhood and slavery by showing how women suffer at the hands of their husbands without legal recourse.[71] Her consistent use of slavery as a metaphor for marriage, well past the Civil

Figure 3.1 *The Freedom Ring* by Eastman Johnson. Reproduction used courtesy of the Hallmark Fine Arts Collection.

War—"Our Slave" and "Mrs. Flint's Married Experience" were both published in the 1880s—suggests a commitment to the issues raised by abolition long after they were fashionable. In this respect, Cooke sees race and slavery as an unresolved conflict in all parts of the United States, not just the "rebel" South.

Indeed, her critique of the patriarchal structure of New England culture, in particular, powers her literary impulse toward the realism her readers most appreciated. Her writings provide readers with a different portrait of the New England that Stowe romanticized in *Old Town Folks* (1869) as "the seedbed of American culture." Rather, the men and women that inhabit the cramped cottages and barren farms of Cooke's fictional world have little left for themselves or their offspring. Cooke's writings give voice to another nineteenth-century reader, one who related more closely to the hard-scrabble existence described in her fiction. The frequent publication of her stories also suggests that this readership shared her passionate rejection of conventional literary techniques—especially those she linked with sentimentalism.

Cooke's attacks of the literary conventions popularized by sentimentalism are a prominent feature of her work; its literary conventions functioned as adversarial features in Cooke's writing. She voiced her frustration with the sentimental tradition in a direct address to her readers: "Forgive me once more [Cooke implores], patient reader, if I offer you no tragedy in high life, no sentimental history of fashion and wealth, but only a little story about a woman who could not become a heroine."[72] Here, ironically casting the lack of sentimentality as a kind of cultural transgression requiring forgiveness, Cooke takes on a comic mode to undermine sentimentalism's claim to structuring the way readers think about relations between the sexes, the races, and the classes. This story features an "unromantic" figure whose name also serves as the title for the story, "Miss Lucinda."[73] In her love for a pet pig and other idiosyncrasies, readers might be reminded of Mary Wilkins Freeman's "A New England Nun." But Cooke's heroine ends up marrying her suitor despite—or rather perhaps because of—their respective oddities.[74] This story demonstrates Cooke's conviction that "nothing in place or circumstance makes romance"; love between two people, just like any other relationship, succeeds only if each shares a mutual respect for the other.[75]

"Miss Lucinda" is just one of many tales that illustrate the lie of domestic bliss, harmony between the sexes, the natural status and disposition of gender and class distinctions as well as the aspirations for a middle-class home as popular norms in the nineteenth century. Drawing on the register of woman's rights, Cooke writes against literary stereotypes by recasting them through the humanitarian realism of the slave narratives.

Marriage, rather than acting as the happy ending of her stories, tends to be the tragic beginning of many. And it is in the depiction of these domestic relations that Cooke makes a claim to realism.

Conclusion: "Let us Be Graphic and Die!"[76]

Rose Terry Cooke—known to literary historians as one of the local colorists—did not venerate tradition or continuity. In story after story Cooke rails against Calvinism, as well as the gender, race, and class stereotypes that comprise the New England tradition through her depiction of silent suffering, parsimonious husbands, and radical women. Her stories typically focus on "women who cannot become heroines" because they refuse the gendered literary stereotypes that construct women as pious, self-sacrificing, and silent—the very stereotypes that define the literary genre for many scholars.[77] Many of her characters are downright ferocious and Cooke painted scenes with a gothic cast so that readers would not mistake a fascination with the past as a veneration of it. These stories offer a counterhistory to students of New England culture and local color fiction.

Unlike other writers who identified with New England local color fiction and took up these same registers, the tension generated out of Cooke's use of competing vocabularies seems to resolve itself in protest *against* New England tradition and cultural practices. Cooke's work, therefore, opposes both the culture it represents and the literary culture from which it springs. Her sketches of New England life are shot through with anti-New Englandism and thus stand apart from those produced by the canonized local colorists, though her writings appeared in the very same publishing venues—oftentimes, right along side them. Thus, a reexamination of Rose Terry Cooke's fiction also offers us an opportunity to re-examine the ways these terms have consolidated our sense of late-nineteenth-century readers' developing literary tastes and the marketplace that produced them.

In October 1864, Cooke wrote to thank her publisher James Fields for sending her a copy of *Emily Chester: A Novel.*[78] In this letter, she expressed the opinion that the novel's author—Anne Moncure Crane Seemuller (1838–1872)—might yet become the much-needed "original woman-author in America," a rank Cooke did not believe she, nor any of the other women writers in her cohort, had reached. She considered herself as a producer of "little prettinesses and commonplaces" more conducive to the short story—a form given over to "us smaller fry who 'swim on bladders,'" staying afloat, it would seem, through the support of the magazines.

Yet Cooke's choice not to leave the lucrative world of magazine publishing and take up the novel form was perhaps the more canny one. Despite the prejudices that ephemeral literature carries with it, eschewing the novelistic form and book publishing in favor of the periodical press was, nonetheless, an effective way to gain a readership. Thus, though Fields succeeded in luring Hawthorne away from magazine publication in the interest of "art," he largely failed in his efforts with Cooke. Cooke's strategy, later articulated by William Dean Howells in "The Man of Letters as a Man of Business," took popularity seriously, understanding that in "the infant industry" of letters, writers must seek magazines as a source of revenue and in order to build a reputation.[79] One simply is not read in novel form alone, unless, of course, a readership is developed through serialization with book publication to follow.

We can find evidence for Howells's assessment in more Ticknor and Fields history. Despite Hawthorne's popularity with the critics, he never achieved popularity with the reading public. Though his move to the novel did little for him financially, his subsequent reputation in the literary canon benefited.[80] And thus we might say, conversely, that is precisely how Cooke's reputation has suffered. Her work remained popular with readerships—and the editors who were there to serve them—but not with the more powerful sources of cultural transmission.

Until recently, Cooke's works have not been republished and thus have not followed other noted trends used to promote the canonized New England writers. "In later years," Michael Winship observes, "these texts were republished in new forms—in pocket editions, in school textbooks, in a set or volume of collected works—that both reinforced and altered public understanding and the evaluation of their worth."[81] The fact that Cooke's works had not been popularized in this fashion may have something to do with her loss of a reading public. After her death, her work was not reprinted until the 1960s and then, most recently, in the collection edited by Elizabeth Ammons as part of an American women writers series put out by Rutgers University Press.

Not surprisingly, it is "How Celia Changed Her Mind" that Elizabeth Ammons has chosen as the title for the collection she edited. In so doing, she has reframed Cooke in our own terms, terms that don't seem entirely consistent with Cooke's efforts to be a popular writer. Or do they? Perhaps by framing Cooke's literary reputation with this radically feminist story, Ammons has repositioned Cooke in the context of our own literary marketplace and in light of our own literary tastes just as Cooke would have done. No longer interested in the several competing and dissonant registers that characterize Cooke's fiction, Ammons's collection streamlines Cooke's vocabulary by selecting stories that reflect a conception of womanhood more consistent with our own than with Cooke's, which was fraught with paradoxes and contradictions. For instance, in an 1886 letter to her publisher, Cooke referred to *Our Famous Women,* the only work to contain a biographical entry on her from her own time, as "a dreadful book about women," but contributed to it just the same.[82] Indeed, she wrote uncharacteristically sentimental entries on Stowe and Spofford for the volume.

Ironically, Ammons's choice to title the collection, "How Celia Changed Her Mind" reflects further on the problems of reception that plague Cooke's status as a writer. By selecting "How Celia Changed Her Mind" as the titular story of the collection, Ammons chose the one story of those included that Cooke did not first publish in a magazine or journal. Thus we catch a glimpse of the way Cooke's work has been Balkanized, both in the past and today. Today, Cooke's work has been relegated to the company of lesser-known women writers of the nineteenth century.

Rose Terry Cooke's work is wrongly neglected, but not because her ideas are consonant with our own as feminists—as the recent reprint of Cooke's stories suggests. Rather, her work should be read within the context of its publication history as a way to understand the complex confluence of forces that gave rise to realism. Thus, teasing out the historical strands that influenced Cooke's rise and fall in the pantheon of nineteenth-century American writers will prompt larger questions about the nature of the mid- to late-nineteenth-century reading audience and the development of the American canon.

The fact that her work appeared in publications founded and edited by people who campaigned on one hand for abolition and on the other hand for the development of local color suggests how these two movements are related.[83] What literary historians have not discussed is the historical coincidence of the popularity of slave narratives with the rise of realism. Noting a shared "register" between the literary style of the slave narratives and Cooke's work as an early example of realism proves fruitful in illuminating this connection.[84] Thus the registers sounded in Cooke's work may also be useful for reexamining the terms in which today's critics conceptualize the ideological landscape of the past. Every discussion of Cooke recognizes to some extent her interest in race, gender, and region; most treat these concepts as central nodes in her work. Looking more carefully at the ways that categories like "race," "gender" and "region" have consolidated critical interpretations of nineteenth-century American culture has been an important part of recent scholarship in helping us understand that these categories are not just linked, but nested.[85]

4

William Dean Howells without his Mustache

William Dean Howells (1837–1920) harbored many of the same attitudes toward literary fashions as did Rose Terry Cooke. As American literature's "dean" of realism, he played a pivotal role in working against writings that "merely tickle our prejudices and lull our judgment, or that coddle our sensibilities, or pamper our gross appetites for the marvelous."[1] He operated as American literature's middle manager from editorial posts first at *The Atlantic Monthly* and later at *Harper's,* bringing works to the public that resisted romance. An admirer of Rose Terry Cooke's artistry, Howells lauded Cooke for her "good ear for Yankee parlance," calling the stories she published "so good that I grieve to have them the least forgotten."[2]

Little did Howells know that it would be only 20 years before he would write to his friend and fellow writer Henry James about his own eclipse. "I am a comparatively dead cult with my statues cut down and the grass growing over them in the pale moonlight," he admitted in 1915. By the time of this remark, the official mustachioed Howells, the genteel man of letters, had been diminished both as a figure of authorship and as a model to other writers. He had become a forgotten relic of a former era.

Willa Cather, some 20 years earlier, had already pronounced him numb if not dead to the literary marketplace. Cather commented, apropos of the publication of *My Literary Passions,* that "'passions,' literary or otherwise, were never Mr. Howells's forte."[3] According to Cather's assessment, the characteristics that Howells's public image cultivated had cordoned him off from the life of letters. Rather than granting him cultural relevance, his reputation as "dean" of American letters, Cather's remark suggests, had become a liability instead of an asset. Howells's loss of status among writers and critics, however, belies the deeper significance of his career in the development of American literature.

Between 1870 and 1895, when Cather made her remark, American literature had undergone a dramatic shift in literary tastes. The aftermath of the Civil War produced a new genre of writing, one that would replace the slave narratives in popularity: the Civil War memoir.[4] Characterized by the same distinct literary features of narrative detail and specificity, the Civil War memoir diverged significantly in that it was a profoundly white genre aimed at reconciliation between the North and South in post-Reconstruction America rather than the radical ideals of racial equality propounded in the earlier era. In speaking of a successful series of Civil War writings published in the popular *Century* magazine, historian David Blight observes, war recollections, unlike their abolitionist counterparts, were used "as a depoliticized vehicle of sectional reconciliation."[5] Race, the central figure in the politics of the earlier era, had lost its fashionable edge. Thus the public came to know realism as a literary genre with its ties to slave narratives eclipsed by the absence of race as a central mode of tension.

Today, we must look closely in order to recover realism's racial traces through its connection to abolitionism. William Dean Howells's ties to abolition ran deep. Raised by an ardently abolitionist family with stakes in print media, Howells cut his editorial teeth on antislavery issues in the *Sentinel,* his father's newspaper.[6] And according to Rodney Olsen, the young Howells's literary ambition was legitimized through the letters, columns, and poems he wrote on behalf of the antislavery cause.[7] Throughout his career, he stayed true to his abolitionist roots by building on the humanitarian realism we saw developing in Rose Terry Cooke's work with an important difference.[8] According to the *New York Times* in 1878, no one "outside of a small and suspicious circle [had] any real interest . . . in the old forms of the Southern question," which would include questions about race and slavery. So rather than be chastised, as William Lloyd Garrison was in this 1878 editorial, for an archaic, unpopular, and even paranoid interest in the social and racial tensions of the Civil War past, Howells created a predominantly white, middle-class fictional world.[9] We will find the key to Howells's transformation of his abolitionist sentiments into middle-class values in the literary marketplace. A close examination of William Dean Howells's career will grant us insight into the deracialization of the humanitarian narrative as it was thoroughly converted into the genre we now know as realism.

Looking through a trove of photographs relating to the life of William Dean Howells (1837–1920) at the Houghton Library, I discovered an envelope marked "William Dean Howells w/o his mustache (see figure 4.1)."[10]

Figure 4.1 William Dean Howells w/o his Mustache. Photograph by permission of the Houghton Library, Harvard University

Taken at the height of his career in 1882, this photograph suggests something about Howells's rise and fall in American letters. A photograph of Howells without his mustache sounded a little like "the emperor without his clothes" to me since the "dean" of American realism is known as a man with a full mustache in good late-nineteenth-century style. On another envelope also marked "WDH w/o his M," his daughter Mildred penned a statement prohibiting the publication of this photograph within the lifetime of Howells's literary heirs. Delving further into the file box, I was drawn to other unfamiliar images, images that contrast with the icon of nineteenth-century authorship William Dean Howells cultivated.

This photograph—and the note inscribed on its envelope—hints at how deeply William Dean Howells's career was imbricated in the conflicting forces of his own time. His success owed much to his skillful manipulation of the boundaries that separated literature from business, nineteenth-century tastes from twentieth-century practices. Just as his work negotiates nineteenth-century literary conventions for the modern sensibility, so, too, does his projected image. This chapter brings William Dean Howells's literary career into contact with the history of his critical reception in order to explore the development of literary production as it responded to and emerged within the context of the literary marketplace—a marketplace saturated with post-Reconstruction racism. A focus on the contrast between the unpublished and published images of Howells provides us with visual evidence of the tension between the business of literature and its subject matter. Linking the public image of Howells with other unpublished material—datebooks, checkbooks, financial accounts, and business contracts—will uncover other aspects made invisible by the construction of William Dean Howells as a figure in American literary history. In this rendering, Howells's career acts as a palimpsest for the hidden story of realism.

My discussion unfolds in four phases—each using a different kind of material data to reckon the meaning of the man behind the mustache. The first section draws on unpublished writings from early journals to set the "rags-to-riches" story of Howells's career into a more complex narrative. In the second section, I study in detail Howells's analysis of his financial situation. The third section focuses on his novelized account of literary publishing in *A Hazard of New Fortunes.* In the final section, I present a comparison of the published and unpublished photographs. This juxtaposition will show Howells's cult status as a careful construction of authorship put into play by the man and solidified by later critics and biographers.

Howells's trademark image has encouraged critics—beginning with Cather—to cordon him off from the contradictions and tensions of the late nineteenth and early twentieth century in the United States. Repositioning Howells within the complex forces at play during his career reveals the shortcomings of the traditional reception of this author's reputation as a writer and as a cultural gatekeeper. Thus this case study of William Dean Howells considers the larger apparatus of literary production within the context of an emerging capitalism as formative in the development of American Literature as a national "trademark." A reexaminination of William Dean Howells's career and writings mirrors the cultural tensions of publishing as it sought to profit from the development of American literary culture as a commodity.

I. The Business of Becoming a Man of Letters

The written records that Howells left behind help identify components of his literary development not evident in the "rags-to-riches" narrative his success suggests. Howells wrote "Mihi cura futuri" (Latin for "my care is for the future"[11]) on the facing page of his datebook for 1860. Looking into the contents of the diary illuminates just what Howells meant by "the future." Within this pocket diary and daily almanac, Howells actually wrote very little. Indeed, he was generally a poor journal keeper, and in this case, there are only a few entries—one on 20 January about the weather (a popular subject for Howells), and another on the celebration of Saint John's day by the freemasons. Unlike his fellow farmers, however, Howells's notations are not consistent enough to form a personal almanac.[12] The several other observations pertain only to his accounts—the details of which are carefully kept in the back of the notebook under the heading "cash accounts."

Howells consistently demonstrates a certain reservation—if not self-consciousness—in keeping journal and diary entries and here, again, he departs from the customary use of diary and journal keeping. In this mode, Howells limits himself to entry after entry on weather conditions and the like. Today's literary historian may be charmed by the youthful flailings of the budding writer who records, "Yesterday got off about 3 o'clock, and took my big kite, made on Thursday night, down to the common to fly it. . . ."[13] This entry goes on to enumerate "feelings which only boys with a good kite can experience"; it is the only one of its length and detail, so the literary historian might find the reading disappointing for its lack of personal ephemera and insight. Revelation, or even exhilaration (of this kind or any other), is rare in this diary. More typically, the entries drone on, until, after a few weeks of this sort of dribble, they start to taper off and fizzle out with remarks such as "Nothing of very great importance today"; and "I did not write in my diary last night, or the night before, because I had nothing to record, and partly because I felt to [*sic*] tired."[14]

At best, one could call these entries sparse and irregular; hardly the sort of thing one would expect of the "dean of American realism." Or is it? There is something about the lack of direction, the nature of boredom, in other words, the journal's sheer humanness, that anticipates the style of the realist Howells would later become. Nowhere does a reader of these early diaries encounter a scrap of the verse that Howells had been busy trying to promote. Rather, these dry entries seem to lumber along, actively resisting the sentimental ethos of his day. By not filling in the gaps of his life with philosophical interpretation and emotional renderings, Howells ignores the possibility of his circumstances as grist for his poetry mill. Instead, as he here describes it, this is the life of the not-yet-professional realist tracking his own expectations not those of the imagined audience. In his refusal to romanticize the drudgery of his daily existence we might recognize his ambition to live beyond his present circumstances. Practicing his signature—which he does repeatedly and with palpable flourish—seems to be the only writerly activity that holds his attention.[15] As in this photograph with his Ohio friends, Howells (center) is already busy preparing his image by practicing his signature "look" (see figure 4.2).

Figure 4.2 William Dean Howells with his Friends 1855. Photograph by permission of the Houghton Library, Harvard University.

As if to explain the nonprofessionalism of the journal, Howells pastes in an article and writes: "The history of the above piece is somewhat eventful. I wrote it one week when I was sick and not at work. I gave it to father, and . . . he gave it to the editor of the *Ashtabula Telegraph,* and they published it . . . Do not know when I shall commence writing regularly in my Journal again." It would seem publication brought about a release from the toil of journal keeping. While it is not known if Howells was actually paid for this article, clearly publication marked a departure for him from the rank and file of typesetter and to the exalted realm of storyteller. The next entry is dated 21 July, several months later. The last entry of the diary reads, "Very hot all day. A little rain this afternoon. Do not know of the least news at present. Have received no letter from any quarter."[16]

In contrast to his habits as a diarist, Howells was always prodigious in his account keeping and in this category his interest clearly quickened. Throughout the journal it appears that the young Howells knows exactly what's missing from his story: money. His financial situation is the only subject treated consistently and in detail in all of his journals and records. Since we now know Howells as having written the father of all American economic novels (*The Rise of Silas Lapham*), we should not be surprised that details abound when it comes to keeping track of his own accounts receivable. As early as 1860, Howells was logging all payments received (including the sources for income) as well as anticipating future revenue. Income sources and accumulated sums seem to command the attention of the young writer and thus provide us with an alternative account of those early days. The diligence Howells shows in his financial records suggests that he had in practice less difficulty reconciling the artist with the businessman than his public persona would have suggested. And, perhaps more significantly, that a monetary account of his progress was more meaningful than the narrative one.

Despite the level of detail in this section of his journal however, there are no entries in the section of the diary called "accounts payable." This is actually quite typical of Howells's bookkeeping. Like Longfellow, Howells shows much more interest in the plus side of his finances than the expenses he incurs; that is: he exhibits a greater concern for his gross rather than his net worth.[17] This pattern remains true in Howells's later financial records as well. In a folder catalogued "Investments and Miscellaneous," one finds Howells assessing his financial status in a series of documents written between 1890 and 1897; among these accounts there is no list of debts.[18]

After his break with the *The Atlantic Monthly* in 1881 and his move to New York in 1889, Howells began, literally, to take stock of his situation as a writer and an entrepreneur in the world of letters. Scholars have been at pains to contextualize this aspect of Howells's literary life. From the moment Henry James first lamented that Howells "with such a pretty art, can't embrace a larger piece of the world," Howells has been chastised for allowing his financial needs to limit his artistic ability. James, and many others since, have noted that Howells, as editor of *The Atlantic Monthly,* and, later, *Harper's,* had, in the words of Michael Anesko, "bartered a certain kind of freedom for the security of the assured publication and a weekly paycheck."[19] What I'd like to look at is how Howells used his accounts as a means to tell his own story and ultimately to form the genre of realism.

In 1890, he records his financial assets in terms of "cash," "real estate," "stocks," and "life insurance." He assesses his estate at $60,000. By 1892, his assets increased by $8,409.81.[20] Besides the increase in funds, there is also another important difference in the way Howells views his assets at this point. Unlike the earlier (and more naïve) record in which amounts were rounded off to the nearest hundred, Howells is now keeping his record to the penny. Here we see Howells implicated in his own "hazard of new fortunes," published in the same year. But success—like desire—remains elusive. On the reverse side of the 1892 assessment, Howells makes a notation about annual income from his literary and real estate investments:[21]

> In addition to this I own about $10,000 of stereotype plates in the house of Houghton, Mifflin, and Co., Boston, and Harper & Bros., New York. But this value is [contingent] on the publisher's right, and could not be negotiated without selling my copyrights to them. My books now bring in say $2000 to $2500 a year in old copyrights. The Cambridge house is let to Arthur—at $800 a year for four years from Sept. 1st.

These notions indicate that Howells had come to value his assessments in terms of their ability to produce; they further evidence his tendency to keep track of accounts receivable as exhibited in the 1860 documents.[22]

Howells's more recent self-evaluation reflects a new-found value in his work-as-text: the stereotype plates that he owned could suddenly take on a value that had been made possible by strides in the legal definition of intellectual property and U.S. copyright.[23] His record of financial assets now regularly includes his literary property as a material asset. By July 1897, in addition to the regular line-up of investments and assets Howells includes $5,000 for plates as part of his financial summary. Howells is no longer adding sums, treating himself as the itinerant wage earner. Yet the haphazard nature of these documents—random sheets of paper with scribbled sums and notations—reflect his tendency to value his assets mainly in their liquid form—as money. In this document, he renders real estate and literary property in equal terms: both are investments that produce an income proportionate to the marketplace.[24] Notably, in the 1897 assessment, Howells, for the first time, lists the Cambridge house at the top and, in the final place previously allotted to his life insurance policy, he now notes "plates, Harper & Bros. and Houghton & Co – 5000.00," as the last entry before he totals the sum.[25] Literary historians are quick to point out Howells's place as one of the leading writers of the literature of economics; as these archival documents show, he was also a pioneer of capitalizing on the economics of literature.

II. Show Me the Money

This new awareness of his literary production *as a financial asset* takes on greater significance when one places Howells in the context of American literature and culture. Ohio-born and raised—he was a newcomer to an old-timer world. Much has been made of Howells's "rise." Like many of his own characters, he managed to climb the social and cultural ladder designed for the New England culture industry. But, unlike so many of his literary characters—Silas Lapham chief among them—he came to be accepted by the Brahman class his books—and his career as a trajectory of the emerging business culture at large—supplanted. What the unpublished material presented here so far suggests is that profits as a measure and condition of success were part and parcel of how Howells viewed himself. Marketability, therefore, played a formative role in the development of his literary career.

Howells was obviously writing for the little guy (or gal)—by aiming for the middlebrow audience of *Harper's* and *Century* with a view toward making a living. And that would explain his avoidance of racial issues in his fiction until the publication of *An Imperative Duty* in 1892 despite his abolitionist background.[26] Contracts held in the archive at the Houghton Library show that Howells regularly took "orders" from editors so that they would meet his price.[27] *The Rise of Silas Lapham,* for instance, was developed in response to specifications laid out by Henry Mills Alden, editor of *Harper's*—the magazine that ran the novel serially before Osgood published it in book form. Alden stipulated—in the contract drawn up by Howells, Osgood, and the Harper's brothers—"that it shall be a story of American life and character with sufficient humor to meet popular requirement and having no such singularity of plot as characterized 'An Undiscovered Country'—i.e., no plot based on exceptional or unusual manifestations of human character."[28] *The Rise of Silas Lapham*—one of Howells's masterpieces—grew out of a creative process set in motion and limited by market demands. The directions to the author set forth by Alden indicate both what the publishers wanted and did not want.

Without having to say it, the terms of this publication contract calling for humor in the treatment of unexceptional and ordinary human qualities precludes the depiction of characters of color as central to the plot.

Instead, the qualities called for here coincide precisely with standards that characterize realism in the United States as stories about white people and their economic hardships. Rather than defer to the "Artist," they insisted that the artist must meet the market's demands. Thus, in order to remain the "man of letters," Howells also had to be a "man of business."[29]

Fortune was certainly—and legitimately—part of the goal of the realist writer. And why shouldn't a "man of letters" also be the "man of business" it seems Howells most consummately was? The last document contained in the investment file is Howells's undated "Income-net." The sum totals at $19,260—I can only assume that is annual.[30]

Figure 4.3

E. 73rd St. house	$1,700
W. 82nd St. house	1,800
Cambridge house	600
Houghton Mifflin & co books	900
Harper & Brothers, new old books	5,000
N. L. Bond	400
P. B.& L. W.	60
Phyllip Co., estimated	1,000
	$11,460
Supposed	10,000
	$21,460
Easy Chair	5,000
	$16,460
Contributions	3,000
	$19,460

According to these calculations, Howells *deducted* the money he would earn from his writings for *Harper's* "Easy Chair." Unless this was an error in arithmetic, Howells plainly valued passive income—generated by investments of both a literary and financial nature—more highly than the salaried income provided by the "Easy Chair" writings. And looking at the bulk of his investments, it is also clear that it was these he was primarily interested in cultivating. By 1908, in addition to the Cambridge house, Howells had stakes in three cooperative apartments in New York City. Tax receipts for 314 West 82nd Street (valued at $25,000), 259 West 85th Street (valued at $23,000) and for 38 East 73rd Street (valued at $38,000) totaling $1,388.08 were all paid by check on 29 Oct 1908.[31] Based on the assessed values, these properties were worth $86,000. What's more, these were paying investments. As the statement of net worth reveals, Howells was getting an income of $3,500 for the two New York properties that were not his residence.[32] Howells secured his investment for the future of

American literature partly by virtue of his interests in business. His assets, not only in cash and stereotype plates but also in ample shares of the real-estate market, demonstrate a canny business sense that would make any one with admiration for the entrepreneurial marvel at the man's resourcefulness. And yet so many scholars and literary historians have had trouble coming to grips with Howells's business acumen as a literary asset. Just as historians have been loathe to recognize the link between liberal capitalism and moral suasion in the antislavery movement as discussed in chapter 1, so, too, have their literary counterparts been reluctant to taint the dean of realism's motivations with the business of making money.

One of the conclusions that all these financial records suggest is that Howells's literary success is inextricably bound up with his business sense. Despite his observation, in the 1902 essay, "The Man of Letters as a Man of Business," that "literature is still an infant industry," he and a few others like him managed to make it a profitable one by playing to the market—a market that had already demonstrated a decided interest in humanitarian issues. Gone was the struggle to end slavery as a vehicle for moral uplift—though Howells did visit the issue of racial prejudice in *An Imperative Duty* (1892). Rather, as we will see in the next section of this chapter, Howells' humanitarian realism made the tensions felt by the business class concerning its ethical responsibilities a focus of his fiction.

Part of what is interesting about Howells is that he also made the pressures of the market a significant part of his writing process. Not only are his best novels known as "economic" ones that develop themes taken from the marketplace, but he also kept himself in the marketplace as a way to ensure productivity. He juggled his artistic goals with his business interests in ways that are central to his conception of the literary man. According to his design, the need to earn money not only promoted literary production, it guaranteed it.

A review of job offers Howells turned down illustrates the importance of financial need in Howells's design. Johns Hopkins University offered Howells a lucrative professorship in 1882—the same year the photo of Howells without the mustache was taken.[33] The offer meant guaranteed income with summers off to write, yet Howells demurred because, as mentor James Russell Lowell put it, "You would have the advantage of fixed income to fall back on. Is this a greater advantage than the want of it would be as a spur to your industry?"[34] Lowell, who complained—loudly—about finances all his life, here seems to be inviting the wolf, not only to the door, but also inside the house as a protection against low productivity! By following Lowell's advice, Howells secured his investment in the future of American literature by applying the law of supply and demand to his writing career. As long as there was a demand for his writing, that would compel him to supply it. Thus, his assets, not only in cash and stereotype plates but also in real estate, are only part of what demonstrate a canny business sense. He used the market—in almost every sense—to further his career.

III. "It's the Greatest Idea . . . Since the Creation of Man"

In *Hazard of New Fortunes* (1890), William Dean Howells boldly moves the literary marketplace out of the hidden margins of his own literary production and into the center of readers' attention as the focus of the novel itself. The novel takes the development of a literary magazine as its locus. At the novel's start, the magazine is in its germination—so early in its development that readers first learn of the magazine as an unnamed business proposition. Referred to only as "it" in the novel's first paragraph, the conception of the magazine promises more than just a salary; those who take it up will get a "share in its success."[35] By the end of the novel, the magazine has made good on its promise. The two characters we meet at the novel's beginning as prospective business manager and literary editor to the magazine have become co-owners and joint operators of the venture. Through the magazine as the novel's central narrative mechanism, Howells explores literary production and its pitfalls from a business perspective.

Howells's interest in how publishing sought to profit from the development of American literary culture spawned a set of characters who represent the competing forces that influence literature as a business. Fulkerson—the novel's prime mover—takes on the business side of the magazine's operation. This character, whose first name is withheld for the entirety of the novel, is the business manager of the magazine, which is called *Every Other Week*.[36] His shameless use of all forms of promotion—from name-dropping to the hyperbole of the marketplace—allows readers to see some of the hazards fortune can bring. In particular, his single-minded devotion to the prospect offered by the literary magazine makes him susceptible to a moral lapse that becomes a central tension in the novel. Fulkerson organizes a banquet to celebrate *Every Other Week* and its contributors. As he brainstorms this occasion, modeled on the author dinners hosted by *The Atlantic Monthly, Harper's* and other literary magazines of the day, he conceptualizes the event entirely in marketing terms. But the occasion turns out to be a social disaster. In calculating the "effects" of the dinner, he failed to consider the event in human terms. Arguments break out as personalities clash and tempers flare. The moral of this story is not that literature must not be conducted as a business but rather that business has something to learn from the novelist who has made the complexities of human relations his or her business.

Fulkerson functions as an important device to tease out the complexities prompted by the subjection of literature to the forces of the marketplace. To help this radical project succeed, however, Howells returns to the fictional couple with whom he began his own career as a novelist: Isabel and Basil March.[37] Howells introduced the Marches to readers in his first novel, *Their Wedding Journey* (1871). Readers are already familiar with the Marches' values and thus their presence helps to sanitize the subject of the novel. Using the Marches as another kind of trademark—this time a fictional one—Howells ensures a degree of stability in a novel that is about the unsteady and shifting forces of the marketplace.

Howells's inclusion of the Marches as a significant feature of the novel plainly forges a connection between this work and that earlier novel. The narrative decision to return to the Marches in *Hazard* also urges readers to connect this work to his other works.[38] Thus, readers might be encouraged to relate the narrative irregularity of the novel—including the much-discussed outsized chapters on apartment hunting and the novel's uneven construction—with Howells's first and ultimately successful novelistic experiment. The fact that Howells returned several more times to this pair in later works makes the relationship between all of these works even more explicit. At the very least, Howells is working a niche market he created with this fictional couple.

In this and Howells's earlier depiction of the Marches, Basil March bears a remarkable resemblance to Howells himself.[39] March, like Howells, wears at least three hats: one as literary editor, another as author, and a third as family man. From the outset, March had been identified as a "natural born literary man" who had eschewed a career as a writer because it wouldn't pay. At the moment when readers are introduced to March, however, he has reached a crossroads in his career. He has decided to leave the insurance business, a career that goes "against the grain" of his "nature." Before, family concerns had kept March away from "early literary ambitions"; instead he insured his family's future by going into the insurance business himself.

In contrast to Fulkerson, the novel thus also offers readers an example of the literary man with a business sense in Basil March. The position of literary editor for *Every Other Week* affords March the opportunity to try his hand at the business of literature by using his literary talent as a guide. The other obstacle (besides money) to fulfilling his long-deferred dream of writing is the necessity that the family relocate from Boston to New York. Making the move a condition of the job allows the narrative to explore still another facet of the changing literary marketplace: regional differences in consumption (in other words, reading). Unlike Boston—where as Howells had observed elsewhere, everyone reads—in New York, as Fulkerson points out, "they don't read much . . . they write, and talk about what they've written."[40] Thus, this literary marketplace has a decidedly different climate than the world he is leaving behind. But it does not take March long to realize that he can (and must) convert the exposure to a new environment and new material into a way to jumpstart his own writerly interests. That he contribute as well as edit is part of the bargain. Thus his living—in another resonance with Howells's career—depends on the joint tasks of literary production and management.

The novel uses its minor characters to explore other hazards that the new fortune of literary publications promise. The characters Alma, Beaton, Lindau, and Dryfoos offer readers glimpses into the various contingencies that affect literary production. Alma, for instance, concludes that marriage and family are off-limits to her as an artist. When presented with the most romantic of possible partners—fellow artist Beaton—as a possible mate, she concludes, "I'm wedded to my art and I'm not going to commit bigamy."[41] Beaton, a gifted artist, is marred by a disgusting degree of selfishness. The narrative notes how he consistently deprives his own father of money owed rather than forego some earthly pleasure such as a glass of port or a new, more fashionable coat. Lindau, a German immigrant who lost his hand fighting for slaves in the Civil War, has made labor inequities his raison d'être. When Lindau finds out that his own paycheck comes from a "dirty" industrialist (Dryfoos) whose fortune was made by labor abuses, he refuses to accept payment. Yet, despite the intensity (and seeming irrationality) of his views, the novel rewards him with an heroic death.[42] Not so for Mr. Dryfoos, the dirty industrialist who provides financial backing for *Every Other Week*. Dryfoos's hubristic attempts to use his money make his ideological beliefs felt through his control over the money are a clear violation of a central tenet of the marketplace. After blundering badly with friends, family, and business associates, he ultimately redeems himself through his handling of the magazine.

The main "character" round which the minor characters swirl is actually the magazine itself. Named for its periodicity—in other words for its very magazineness—*Every Other Week* distinguishes itself from its competitors through management practices as well as the material it publishes. Arguing against the usual practice of commissioning works by well-known writers and artists, Fulkerson calls it "all wrong," even "suicide." What Fulkerson terms "suicide," he also links to a form of literary degeneration. By repeatedly publishing the same writers, he argues, the health of literature is threatened by the lack of selective pressure in Darwinian terms. As the same *writers* produce the same *writing,* they intellectually and commercially deaden literature—both its producers and consumers. Organized *against* the very principle of name recognition, or trademarking, that publishers—and Howells himself—depended on as a central marketing devise, Fulkerson insists that the magazine must promote itself through the use of unknown writers. "Names! Names! Names! . . . the new fellows have no chance," he exclaims.[43]

The novel makes it plain that Fulkerson's commitment to "new blood" does not signal a return to the gentleman writer—an amateur ideal of authorial anonymity that dominated the literary field of an earlier epoch.[44] On the contrary, Fulkerson's prophylactic against a kind of literary inbreeding is another feature of modern capitalism: the marketplace itself. Contributors will be paid in proportion to the sales of the magazine—not according to some arbitrary price set by the whim of the publisher *or* author. The magazine will restore "the good old anonymous system, the only fair system," to publishing practices.[45] As plans to put these ideals into practice come to fruition, Fulkerson likens the innovation to the "idea of self-government in the arts," concluding that "it amounted to something in literature as radical as the American Revolution in politics."[46]

The model for this literary enterprise, however, resists the conventions that gave rise to William Dean Howells's own literary career. Ironically, Howells's success owes much to the use of "names!" as Fulkerson deploys the term in his expletive. Features such as the list of contributors and the woodcut of the author and a recurring set of characters—such as Isabel and Basil March were for Howells—helped establish the writer as recognizable—identifiable traits that register as a "trademark" of sorts.

Reading *A Hazard of Fortunes* in light of Howells's experiences as both editor and author, this novel offers readers a blueprint for radical change—changes Howells endorses in this fictional account of the literary marketplace. In the novel—unlike in life—Howells openly celebrated the skills required for literary success.[47] Fulkerson, March, and their magazine survive due to strategic manipulations of the boundaries that separated literature from business, nineteenth-century tastes from twentieth-century practices. The magazine's collective identity—as a source of new and exciting material from a variety of sources—replaces earlier formations of the literary from the coterie of authorship to the name-brand recognition of celebrity writers. These forms of success give way to the next wave of capitalism achieved through the corporate management of Fulkerson and March. Their careful manipulation of the magazine's image—rather than that of the author—refocused (ideally, at least) attention on the literary product and away from its producer. An examination of the photographic history of Howells's own career embodies the tradition the managers of *Every Other Week* sought to overturn.

IV. William Dean Howells Without his Mustache

Beginning with the advent of the daguerreotype, images of authors became central to the promotional efforts associated with professional authorship. In addition to books, publishers advertised likenesses of their most popular authors for sale. By the 1880s, engravings of authors—taken from photographs—formed a significant part of a reader's impression both of the writer and his or her work.[48] Success as a writer was often accompanied by celebrity.[49] Manipulating the visual image of the writer, therefore, becomes a component of promoting the literary work itself. As we've seen in the use of frontispieces in the slave narratives, portraits of the author carefully construct the authors as emblems of literary works; they act as a visual preface to and trademark of the literary text.

The care with which authorship is constructed through visual images of the writer becomes even more evident as other images come to light. The images discarded and/or passed over by publishers, biographers, and literary historians offer a glimpse into the criterion for selection and the standard features of what authors, publishers, biographers, and literary historians have considered to be the "mark" of authorship. Images such as the one of Howells without his mustache stand out because they do not contain the conventional signifiers (see figure 4.1). The note accompanying the 1882 photograph that I found at the Houghton library can serve as evidence that Howells and his literary heirs consider the mustache such an important feature of his literary identity that he did not want to be seen without it.

Another photograph we might turn to is one of the straw-hatted Howells, taking a break from the heat of the day in Saratoga (see figure 4.4). This photograph brings us into contact with the casual Howells, and despite the fact that he's looking directly at us, he's less "posed" than is typical of the photographs biographers and literary historians reproduce. This is a "snapshot"—not a "portrait" with Howells at its center—and thus affords us a glimpse into an alternative Howells. He's a little tired and sweaty—like most tourists—and this is part of what makes him seem ordinary. Interestingly, however, this—like the photograph of Howells without his mustache—is not the Howells presented for posterity by previous biographers and literary historians. Both of these images undermine Howells's status as "dean" by presenting him as—recalling the terms of the contract for *Silas Lapham*—an example of neither the "exceptional" nor the "unusual."

Taken around the same time as the photograph in Saratoga, the next photograph shows Howells even more unbuttoned (see figure 4.5). Despite the presence of books, paper, and an inkstand that suggest the writer's work, we do not see Howells at work. Relaxing while he giddily pours

Figure 4.4 Straw-hatted Howells (1894). Photograph by permission of the Houghton Library, Harvard University.

himself a drink in his Kittery Point library, he might be seen as inviting the viewer to enjoy an afternoon cocktail along with him. Through his gesture and apparel, Howells reinforces the ordinary quality of middle-class living so characteristic to his fiction.

This photograph departs significantly from the "writer at his desk" genre in which the desk plays an important role in establishing the writer as both serious and professional. Perhaps because Howells is not seated at

Figure 4.5 William Dean Howells, Kittery Point (1894). Photograph by permission of the Houghton Library, Harvard University.

it, this desk fails to mark the subject as a writer. Howells's professional identity and professional stature, in this photo, is only recognizable through the viewer's prior knowledge of his reputation.

Now, I'd like to compare these to the frequently reproduced portraits of Howells. Reproduced in most biographies, this photograph introduces us to William Dean Howells, literary novice, with two friends in 1855 (see figure 4.2).[50] Perhaps part of what attracts biographers to this photograph is the contrast between Howells and his companions. Howells—in the center—exudes refinement and respectability to the point of smarminess. The well-coifed hair of this compact figure suggests Boston refinement; he might be here visiting these rough-hewn Ohio frontier friends on a civilizing mission.[51] Howells would later write in "American Literary Centers" that it was Boston that "in my time at least, had a distinctly literary atmosphere, which more or less pervaded society."[52] In Boston, Howells soliloquized, "there was not only such a group of authors as we shall hardly see here again for hundreds of years, but there was such regard for them and their calling, not only in good society, but among the extremely well-read people of the whole country as Boston once did through writers whom all the young writers wished to resemble."[53] His dark suit and steady gaze reflect his esteem for Boston and the young writers he not only wished to resemble, but expressly wanted to become. His appearance prompts the viewer to recognize the difference between him and his companions whose visual clues—from their hairstyles to the sharp contrasts of their clothes—suggest the bustle and energy of the frontier. This photograph reinforces Howells as an emblem of New England culture. Despite the fact that he has yet to leave the frontier that raised him, Howells magically has assumed the air of Boston respectability—especially when compared to his Ohio friends.

Another photograph popular with biographers and literary historians presents the dapper Howells, in a black derby, ready to assume his post as U.S. Consulate in Venice, Italy in 1861 (see figure 4.6). Here he appears in the garb of the artist, sporting a cape. He has already raised the mustache that will become synonymous with the author. These photographs suppress the midwestern boosterism that the early diaries reflect.

A reward for a successful campaign biography of Lincoln, bestowal of the consulate on Howells recognizes his ability to craft a public image out of homespun details. The consulate permitted Howells to marry and start his career as a writer. He later explained to readers in *My Literary Friends and Acquaintances* that his move into the literary profession was well thought out. He chose travel sketches primarily because this was an area that was not dominated by the literary giants of his day—Hawthorne, Longfellow, and Lowell. Throughout his career, Howells returned to the tried-and-true form; much of his novel-writing and many of his early fictions have travel as their central novelistic mechanism. Early titles such as *Venetian Life* (1866) and *Italian Journeys* (1867) take travel as their subject while introducing readers to everyday experiences. Howells had brought the popular travel sketch model he had perfected to bear on the novelistic successes such as *Our Wedding Journey* (1872) and *A Chance Acquaintance*

Figure 4.6 William Dean Howells (1861)

(1873).[54] These works, like the photographs we've just looked at, have come to define the young writer.

One of the things the early photographs and writings have in common is the degree to which Howells sought the identifying marks of professionalization. All accounts of Howells's career agree that he was drawn to the literary at a young age. What has been discussed only re-

Figure 4.7 Boston Study

cently, however, is Howells's selection of Boston as his professional launching point.[55]

Later photographs of the writer tend to reinforce writing as a profession and Howells as one of its most professional practitioners. Here is Howells at his desk in Boston (see figure 4.7).

Figure 4.8 New York Study

Hunched over his desk, Howells is too busy writing to greet the viewer. Although the scene bears some class markers, it does not suggest wealth as much as it does the writer's work. Closely cropped and tightly focused, the photograph fixes its subject in what seem to be cramped quarters. The composition of this photograph restricts the viewer to the element of Howells's life related to his work as a professional author; it confirms the ethic of work and respectability epitomized by the Boston literary scene.[56]

Though in the next photograph Howells is seated at the same desk, the emphasis is neither on him nor his writing. Taken after his move to New York, this photograph presents a different view of Howells (see figure 4.8).

Sitting back, arm draped over the chair, Howells rests on his accomplishments as he looks into the viewer's eyes. In its projected comfort and confidence, this photograph relays an important distinction between the Boston Howells and the New York Howells. Howells summed up the difference between these two locations when he noted, "in Boston literature had vastly more honor," while New York is "a vast mart." Aside from Howells and his desk, these two photos have little in common. Though the furnishings are largely the same, little about the mood of the two scenes is. Here, Howells is one object among many in a well-appointed study. This photo invokes a sense of wealth and commodity; Howells's presence in it suggests that authorship is a means to riches. The photograph confirms

Howells's view that in New York "literature is one of the things marketed here; [the city] does not care nearly so much for books as for horses or for stocks."[57] In this New York photograph of the writer at his desk, Howells cultivates the appearance of wealth and leisure—a condition that is confirmed by his posture in this photograph in which he is unencumbered by the travails of writing.

Taken together and measured against each other, these images describe the tension between the components that Howells used to build his image and the image itself. And that's what I realized at the Houghton Library when I saw Howells without his mustache staring back at me. It was at that moment that Howells's struggle to become a literary giant turned vivid. There he was, as an "outsider"—without his mustache magically reconverted back to an ordinary man from Ohio.

▣ ▣ ▣ ▣ ▣

Through the comparison of unpublished photographs, journals, diaries, financial records, and business contracts with the published photographs and writings we are granted multiple views of Howells at rest from his own efforts to produce an acceptable cultural image—one that was free of the hustle and grime of capitalism. These documents also help us see the degree to which Howells (and his literary heirs) participated in and perpetuated that image.[58] The mustache here becomes—like the desk—a signifier for the tradition, prestige and legitimacy that Howells desperately sought. Ultimately, the mustache was also the only remaining visible link to Howells's abolitionist past. Despite several breakdowns, indicators of the degree of anxiety Howells felt as he pursued his goals, Howells continued his "struggle upwards," working within the confines of a literary marketplace conditioned by rampant racism and a sentiment of reunion. Looking at the 1882 photo of Howells "without his mustache" again allows us to see how the missing mustache unsettles the narrative of (white) privilege—at least enough to have his literary heirs withhold permission to publish it.

The image of Howells without his mustache departs from the image of the moneyed, literary man of leisure that previously had populated the pantheon of American writers. This photo calls attention to Howells's transitional status. Just as his work negotiates nineteenth-century literary conventions for the more modern sensibility of the twentieth century, so, too, does his projected image. The mustache locks him into the nineteenth century construction of a gentleman, one peculiar to the century.[59] And the photographs consistently selected to represent the writer underscore the sense that Howells is established, enduring, and traditional—a symbol of white power.

Yet the unpublished archival material presented here tells a different story—one not easily reconciled to a single narrative of success (or failure). Rather, these materials testify to the hard work and constant effort that brought about Howells's success in the literary marketplace of his day. Being compelled to make himself recognizable in popular terms, however, did not still the longing for social justice he was raised to value. Rather, his move toward the life of the gentleman writer in which he valued his passive income over the money he made in "wages," granted him the freedom to play an active role in forming literary tastes. Over time, Howells came to place more financial value on his passive income—royalties, paying investments, and real estate—than he did on earned income from editorial work. These records demonstrate a move away from the "wage-earner" he famously described in "The Man of Letters as a Man of Business" to the man of property—and therefore of power. Paradoxically, Howells's journey to success was consistent both with the nineteenth-century concept of gentleman writer encouraged by his trademark mustache as well as with the newer modes of fluid capital as a signifier of manhood.

Howells's business contracts spin yet another storyline. Howells used the demands of the professional author and editor for both *The Atlantic Monthly* and *Harper's* to keep himself in tune with the marketplace that constructed his image. In turning down offers to teach at both Harvard and Johns Hopkins, Howells eschewed the role of the "guardian figure" in exchange for the "conversational partnership" with his readers that a successful publishing career in his transitional era required. He could attend to the future of American literature best, these professional decisions suggest, from the authorial and editorial chairs available rather than the professorial ones offered to him.

Literary history attests to the many uses Howells made of his power as American literature's middle manager; through his efforts he encouraged a nascent form of what we might call multiculturalism in American literature. After all, Howells had a hand in the careers of writers such as Abraham Cahan, Charles Waddell Chesnutt, Paul Lawrence Dunbar, Sarah Orne Jewett, and Mary Murphree as well as a host of others. This glimpse of Howells as literary entrepreneur should compel us to adjust our lens still again—and in this book at least—one last time. We must now look upon the mustachioed icon known as William Dean Howells with the knowledge we have accumulated from a guided tour through his personal archive coupled with what we've discovered about the historical links between abolition and realism. The image that he cultivated has more to do with a kind of marketing than it does with a conventional notion of the author's identity. Taken together, these archival records show the care Howells took in constructing himself in the image of the nineteenth-century man of letters through twentieth-century means of fluid capital and for twentieth-century purposes. Howells's choice to be perceived as a man of letters while fostering the image through a canny business sense repositions him as a product of twentieth-century America masquerading as a nineteenth-century relic. It is in this hidden history that we can best see Howells's relationship to an earlier group of authors—the slave narrators—who made their stories a source of cultural and literary legitimacy through the introduction of the financial need as a signpost of personal and political struggle.

The Manner of the Marketplace

Edith Wharton as a Race Writer

It is well known that Edith Wharton took an active interest in the design and marketing of her books. I begin with this fact in order to consider the ways in which Wharton's canny business sense dovetails with her contribution to realism. A professed admirer of William Dean Howells's two most popular economic novels, *A Modern Instance* and *The Rise of Silas Lapham,* Wharton made money and the marketplace central themes in her work.[1] Keeping in mind that realism is the genre of the marketplace and that Wharton demanded she be viewed as a realist, in this chapter I illustrate Wharton's relationship to the reform principles at the heart of the humanitarian tradition that grew out of the slave narratives.

Damning Howells for his "incurable moral timidity" when it came to exacting the tragic implications of life as he portrayed it, Wharton was not one to spare her characters. Perhaps the most celebrated example of Wharton's ruthless referendum on the failings of the leisure class can be found in her 1905 bestseller *The House of Mirth.* Ruling that "a frivolous society can acquire dramatic significance only through what its frivolity destroys," Wharton sacrificed her much beloved character to make a point. Nonplussed by Howells's observation that "what the American public wants is a tragedy with a happy ending," Wharton ended the novel with the death of its main character, Lily Bart.[2]

An analysis of this novel about the social downfall of the twenty-nine-year-old Lily Bart brings together race, realism, and the marketplace, the three prongs of my study, perfectly. First, *The House of Mirth* is decidedly concerned with the generic problems associated with realism.[3] The novel is also strangely racial—as many critics have discovered.[4] Further, the book's popularity allows us to consider it as a mirror of a larger cultural consciousness—one that has its roots in abolition in the United States. In what follows, I will pursue these three strands to reflect on how Wharton's work may be seen as an emblem of—to use one of her own titles—"The Custom of the Country," a custom with its roots in realism, race, and the marketplace. Thus my discussion will move back and forth between specific points in the larger project and a rendering of Wharton's place in it.

I. Realism and Readership: Wharton's Transformation of Genre

Perpetually billed as the "lady novelist" because of her family's prominence and wealth, Edith Wharton knew that the social and financial world she operated in and wrote about was never concerned with the "man with the dinner pail" as was the fashion in fiction at the time.[5] Yet, she did consider her work as part of the trend toward veracity in fiction we call realism. Wharton once admitted to a friend that "the assumption that the people I write about are not 'real' because they are not navvies and char women" irked her almost as much as being billed as James's protegee.[6] She insisted, "I write about what I see, what I happen to be nearest to," wryly concluding that her choice of subject "is surely better than doing cowboy chic."[7] Why, Wharton seems to be asking, is writing about one class more legitimate—generically and culturally—than writing about another? Wharton's claims to realism lie as much in our acceptance of this class of people as suitable for a realistic treatment as in the fact that through characterization and plot she follows the conventions of realism in her treatment of old New York society in *The House of Mirth.*

Wharton played to the marketplace without sacrificing her subject—old New York—to the popular taste for Main Street. Realism—in Wharton's mind—had been unfairly appropriated for the representation of the lower classes. Both her critique of the taste for realism and her demand that she be viewed as a realist hinge on class. By incorporating the racist views that undergirded popular notions of class, Wharton adapted realism to suit her narrative purposes.[8] Just as many abolitionists were eager to sever connections between the fight against slavery and wage-labor disputes in an earlier era, Wharton sought to loosen the bond between realism as a tool for social justice and the lower classes. Coding race as a class attribute, Wharton was able to turn her gaze on the upper classes—the group she famously called "a frivolous society"—through the use of realism's tools. As a result, the novel taps into questions raised by eugenics and the emerging field of anthropology.[9] Ironically, her chronicle of the last of a dying race is for a community of readers who hoped to occupy the places left empty by their demise. Thus the novel achieved popularity with a wide readership.

My study of literary history tells me that Wharton's inscriptions of race has its roots in an earlier literary marketplace. Yet, Lily Bart's literary ancestor is not her racial counterpart, the sentimental (white) heroine. Rather, startling as it may seem, Lily Bart's literary roots return to the tragic mulatta figure made famous by Harriet Beecher Stowe's "Eliza," a pivotal character in her record-breaking *Uncle Tom's Cabin.* Despite the fact that Wharton (and her mother!) condemned Stowe for writing "a novel with a purpose," Wharton never hesitated to mention when discussing Stowe how her novel achieved "immensely remunerative results."[10]

Building on such earlier uses of race as a central signifier of class status, its presence in Wharton's work insures her success with a popular audience, with a difference. In her own time, Wharton was influenced by Darwinian theories of culture—and used them to fuel her critique of upper-class practices. Her regard for evolutionary thinkers is well documented. She wrote, in *A Backward Glance,* of "the wonder-world of nineteenth-century science," specifically mentioning work by "Huxley, Herbert Spencer, Romanes, Haeckel, Westermarck, and the various popular exponents of the great evolutionary movement."[11] We also know that Wharton had all of Darwin's works in her library and that she used one of his titles, *The Descent of Man,* to name a collection of her own short stories published in 1904, the year before *The House of Mirth.*[12] Augmenting the social Darwinian notions circulating in her time with her own understanding, Wharton scripted class in racial terms, thus making Lily Bart's struggle "real" to a range of readers that amazed even her.

Wharton often urged readers to "turn to the past to learn what [the] permanent values are in the field of fiction" and praises the novelist for "the incessant renovation of old types by new creative action."[13] What we see in Wharton's transformation of what had become the archetypical mulatta figure is her effort to modify this old type and thus pour "new life" into old forms.[14] Nineteenth-century American novelists used "blood" as a metaphor for race. The presence of white "blood" in a character, according to the nineteenth- and early-twentieth-century racial theory, "elevated" a slave's status in the minds of white slave owners, and later, white employers. The light-skinned mulatta became the archetypical house servant, enslaved or free. Her lighter skin indicated the presence of "white" blood, and thus suggests that she is more "refined" than her darker-skinned sisters.[15] Thus Harriet Beecher Stowe heightened her character Eliza's appeal by according her mulatta status just as Wharton has by coding Lily with these same ambivalent features.

And perhaps the key to the connection between Lily Bart and her literary predecessor is Wharton's much discussed use of "blood." Figures that conform to this literary type are distinguished by the play of "blood" on aspects and events in their lives. "Blood" figures as an explanatory element in a character's fate. In particular, "blood" could account for class standing, physical appearance, and psychological disposition. Wharton drew on "blood" as a figure of character development to represent Lily Bart. Of course, the aspect that is most crucial to the literary stereotype and the character of Lily Bart, however, is the issue of social refinement or class.

Wharton makes use of the association of skin color with class characteristics by coding her "lower class" or "vulgar" characters with a darker or ruddy complexion.[16] Just as Gus Trenor closes in on Lily in his empty townhouse, "he rose, squaring his shoulders aggressively, and stepped toward her with a reddening brow."[17] When he realizes that Lily will not satisfy his desires, "Trenor's face darkened with rage." To be sure that we understand the association of skin color with race, the report continues after a semicolon with, "her abhorrence had called out the primitive man."[18] Wharton thus links Trenor's darkened color with the social characteristics used to stereotype people of color. Elsewhere characters darken, redden, and become ruddy as desire gets the better of their social skills. George Dorset, another would-be lover of Lily Bart, shows this tendency well. Just as he is about to do something "vulgar" his complexion, too, darkens. By stipulating changes in complexion as a signifier of something "bad," Wharton accesses long-time associations of people of color with sexuality, and sexuality with the lower classes.

Class is the defining element in mulatta identity then, not a dark complexion; class determines and negotiates her identity among both blacks and whites. But the tragic mulatta literary stereotype consists of four other features as well—physical beauty, divided nature, unsuitability for slavery, and an inevitable death—all of which also constitute Lily Bart's characterization. The tragic mulatta is always identified with an uncanny beauty, a beauty that somehow manages to seal her fate. Whether it be the cause for unwanted male attention or simply a quality that adds irony to her degraded state, the tragic mulatta's beauty contributes to the second element of her representation. The tragic mulatta is made tragic, in part, by the duality in her "nature." Because she is neither black nor white, or she is both black and white, she has no stable place within either community. Her divided nature often leads to the ironic realization of her slave status. She seems wrongfully enslaved because she is so unlike her fellow slaves. Or, more to the point, her lighter complexion and remarkable beauty point out an uncomfortable resemblance to her mistress. Her remarkable beauty, grace, and class make her slave status an injustice greater than that of other slaves who are not as exceptional as she. Compounded by her divided self, her wrongful placement among the ranks of "low" characters paves the way for the last stock feature of her representation. She dies, either by her own hand or some fatal accident. In either case, there is a strong sense that her death is inevitable. Lily Bart's story reads as if she were a tragic mulatta, right down to her sudden demise.

While everyone in the novel recognizes Lily's beauty, its uncanny nature is most poignantly remarked on by the two men who are in love with her, Lawrence Selden and Simon Rosedale. Both men see this attribute as a key to Lily Bart's tragic status. Selden reflects that, "as she moved beside him, with her long light step, Selden was conscious of taking a luxurious pleasure in her nearness: in the modeling of her little ear, the crisp upward wave of her hair . . . and the thick planting of her straight black lashes."[19] His examination of Lily's physical beauty is oddly specific and technical; the care he takes to describe her physical attributes smacks of the anthropologist—a discipline newly born during Wharton's writing life. His desire to know if her hair was "ever so slightly brightened by art" would seem to be motivated by his interest in her biological inheritance rather than by a false claim to the beauty that she so plainly possesses.[20] Selden's attention, characteristic more of the scientist than the lover, represents the breeder's interest in good stock more clearly than the romantic's rhapsody.

Perhaps more sensitive to reading racial traits on the body from personal experience, Sim Rosedale reacts to the surprise of Lily's power to attract him with a slightly different mindset. "As she leaned back before him," he observed,

> her lids drooping in utter lassitude, though the first warm draught already tinged her face with returning life, Rosedale was seized by the poignant surprise of her beauty. The dark pencilling of fatigue under her eyes, the morbid blue-veined pallor of the temples, brought out by the brightness of her hair and lips, as though all her ebbing vitality were centered there. Against the dull-chocolate-coloured background of the restaurant, the purity of her head stood out as it never had done in the most brightly lit ballroom. He looked at her with a startled uncomfortable feeling, as though her beauty were a forgotten enemy that had lain in ambush and now sprang at him.[21]

This lengthy meditation demonstrates that a racial fantasy activates Rosedale's desire. He does not fail to notice the "purity" of Lily's head, now brought out to greater effect against the "dull-chocolate-coloured background" of these mean circumstances. He is impressed by her power to flourish in an unhealthy—because it is unfamiliar—environment. And Selden's "confused sense" of Lily's beauty finds its counterpart in

Rosedale's "startled uncomfortable feeling." Though Rosedale's response registers fear of Lily's beauty as if it had the power to "ambush" him, both men respond to her looks on a purely racial level. Almost as if her beauty were calibrated to attract and entrap them—whether an unexplained phenomenon as it is for Selden or an attacking enemy in Rosedale's case—Lily's beauty affects both men as an alarming power that threatens to undo them.

But Lily's tragic status has everything to do with divisions within her own nature. Such an unmistakably divided self is consistent with tragic mulatta representation. At a crucial moment when Lily is about to finalize her engagement to Percy Gryce—an engagement that would take her off the marriage "market"—we see another aspect of Lily's tragic flaw. She is at cross purposes, in conflict with herself. Mrs. Carry Fisher describes her nature thus: "That's Lily all over"; she later confides to Selden. "She works like a slave preparing the ground and sowing her seed; but the day she ought to be out reaping the harvest she over-sleeps herself and goes off to a picnic."[22] Her personality is strangely doubled as this example shows; her behavior exhibits the social functions of both the slave and the mistress. Lily is like the tragic mulatta bred to have rich tastes, but destined to be denied the privilege to satisfy them.

Lily chafes as what Selden later calls the "shackles" of her identity. In full recognition of her indentured status, Lily terms her fate not "free"[23] and expresses her longing "to drop out of the race and make an independent life for herself."[24] She knows that not only her lifestyle, but life itself will end as soon as she is no longer a servant to the wishes of others. She realizes that "when she ceased to amuse Judy Trenor and her friends she would have to fall back on Mrs. Peniston." Not one for self-delusion, Lily "saw only the future of servitude to the whims of others, never the possibility of asserting her own eager individuality."[25] Conditioned by the "type" her race and class assign, Lily Bart develops as a character in the context of her servitude.

The irony of her slave status is further developed by the conventions of her dress. The sapphire bracelet that she wears, for instance, confirms her slave status for Selden. The bracelet is a sign that "she was so evidently the victim of the civilization which had produced her, that the links of her bracelet seemed like manacles chaining her to her fate."[26] And, of course, Lily's beauty highlights the ironic status of her enslavement; these qualities distinguish her from what Selden calls "the herd of her sex."[27] Because she is so refined, this logic asserts, she deserves greater freedom to express and extend that refinement. The contradiction between potential and realized qualities gives way to the internal conflict from which her personality suffers and provides further evidence that she is wrongly placed.

Wharton's references to the tragic mulatta increase in subtlety as the novel extracts features that identify the mulatta with commodified servitude. For instance, the tableau vivant, a central scene in the novel, can be read as Wharton's appropriation of the slave sale scene, another standard feature of tragic mulatta fiction. With links to literary, artistic, and popular sources, the tableau vivant form is a kind of cultural amalgamation.[28] And the mixed nature of Lily's display seems to register quite palpably on her viewers. Reactions ranging from disdain and shock to admiration and jealousy ripple through the gathered viewers. In case readers are confused by the variety of reactions, Wharton makes sure we recognize the tableau's reference to the slave sale by having Lily's cousin, Jack Stepney, object to Lily's display "as if she were up at auction."[29] Two other reactions from male viewers register the slave context significantly. Both Gus Trenor and Sim Rosedale react to Lily's display with a frantic sense of impending sale. All resolve to close the deal either by means of rape (Trenor) or marriage (Rosedale and Selden). And it doesn't seem coincidental that the next night Lily is invited to dance to plantation music in Carrie Fisher's studio.[30]

The real clincher of Lily's tragic status, however, is Lily's death. A surprise to readers then and now, why must Lily die? A tropological equivalent to Wharton's use of ellipses in *Ethan Frome,* among other texts, the mulatta symbolizes racial and cultural mixing in Edith Wharton's fiction. Mulattas appear elsewhere in Wharton's fiction symbolizing stress in the social fabric: notably, answering the door of the abortionist's clinic in *Summer,* and sneering at Newland Archer in *The Age of Innocence* as he arrives at Granny Mingot's to give May up.[31] But what drew Wharton to the mulatta figure in the first place? Traditionally, the figure was designated to forge a bond between white readers and the black population struggling for emancipation. The fact that these figures have some "white" blood established a biological relationship to the white reader that could not be denied. Having established this connection, novelists went on to ponder other, deeper and culturally significant similarities between the members of the two races that would wreak havoc with essentialist distinctions. Like her predecessors, Wharton turned to this style of representation in order to tap a reader who might otherwise not care about Lily Bart's predicament—those masses of readers who sent her those "funny" letters and bought 100,000 copies of the novel. Lily Bart's "mulatta" status prevents her story from being "classed" out of realism, keeping *The House of Mirth* in the realist market. And in so far as Lily Bart is a mulatta, she must die.

Wharton's success can be measured in terms of the reaction that Lily Bart's death provokes, then and now.[32] Wharton sought to capture a market of readers that might aspire to break into the ranks that were so carefully guarded by people such as Percy Gryce and others. This is where

Wharton exhibits her canny market sense: Implicit within correspondence between the mulatta stereotype and the protagonist of *The House of Mirth* is the obvious difference between the mulatta and Lily Bart. Lily Bart is a white woman caught in a class struggle—a struggle whose outcome will raise the question as to whether class is inherited and essential, or whether it can be purchased and is, therefore, socially constructed—a burning question to the masses of Americans struggling to establish themselves and their families as members of the American "race." Like so much race fiction, this novel interrogates distinctions between essentialism and social construction in order to leave the question unresolved. After realizing that such distinctions were untenable, Wharton found a disturbingly unstable paradigm of identity in their wake, and the main character of this novel bears the trace of this knowledge in her name. Lily, named after a flower that represents racial and sexual purity is "like a water-plant in the flux of tides."[33] Her demise is accomplished in part to mask the deterioration of the racial and sexual purity her name signifies. She cannot survive in a culture whose values are in flux.

At the same time, the figure of Lily Bart expressed fears of cultural and class change taking place in turn-of-the-century America. In terms with which Wharton herself was familiar through her study of Darwin and others, we can say that there was a kind of biological and cultural amalgamation going on within the New York-based upper classes and it would be a troubling notion to someone like Wharton, whose prejudices are well known. The fact that Lily would have been willing to make a match with Rosedale in a desperate attempt at self-preservation is good evidence of the kind of move that would lead to racial mixing, another kind of "racial suicide." And Lily's theory that Percy Gryce and his ilk yearn for "a creature of a different race,"[34] turns out to be her most egregious error in logic. She did not realize that marriage practices in this tribe are deeply endogamic until Gryce chooses Evie Van Osbourgh as his mate and thus "Gryce's millions . . . joined . . . another great fortune."[35] This moment in the novel mirrors "old" New York's failed efforts to resuscitate itself. Sacrificing the mores that made it "high," it opened its doors to the new "breed" they called "nouveau riche." What had been strictly regulated according to the paradigm of race now became a class that one could aspire to and ultimately join as long as one could successfully imitate its customs.

II. Figures in White: The Racial Nature of Class

Edith Wharton's relation to the topic of race begins with her chosen subject, New York society. After her first novel, *The Valley of Decision,* was published in 1902, Henry James, in one of literature's most famous pieces of advice, adjured Wharton to "do New York." James's advice was belated; yet his words are intriguing in part because Wharton did not need them.[36] Her interest had already returned to her native land; she was at work on "Disintegration," a novel set in New York. Wharton knew that she was better off, as James put it, in her "native pastures," to draw on what was "natural" to her imagination. In Wharton's own estimation, old New York was as much "in her blood" as it was in her experience. She observed that "fate had planted me in New York, and my instinct as a storyteller counseled me to use the material nearest to hand, and most familiarly my own."[37] Here Wharton asserts that she "grew" (like Topsy just grew?) out of her native habitat.

Wharton's connection between the location of her birth and her identity—her social geography[38]—is only part of her racialized sense of class. Born and raised in the New York society that played so important a role in her fiction, Wharton had been, in her own words, "steeped [in it] from infancy."[39] Both her "blue blood" parents, Lucretia and George Frederic Jones, descended from the "best" families; they introduced her into a world that was as rarefied as it was codified. For instance, in her first novelistic attempt, child Edith's protagonist declares to an unexpected guest that, had she known she was to have a visitor, she would have tidied up the drawing room. Instead of being charmed by her daughter's early sense of household responsibility, Lucretia Jones snapped, "Drawing rooms are always tidy."[40] With that she closed the subject. Her mother's repressive response was typical of the society as Wharton first knew it, and Wharton's subsequent critiques reflect the harshness of her initial experiences.

Modern readers greet Lucretia Jones's oft repeated criticism of little Edith's novel writing with astonishment at her lack of maternal pride. She may have been appalled at little Edith's appropriation of mock-class attributes promulgated by popular literary conventions. But more importantly, by condemning the hyperfictional representation of class, Mrs. George Frederic Jones was doing what she thought was exactly the right thing for her daughter Miss Edith Newbold Jones: She was instructing her in the customs and ways of her race.[41] And, as many scholars have observed, a heightened sense of racial survival permeates the atmosphere in which Wharton grew up and lived. A dinner guest at Theodore Roosevelt's inauguration celebration in 1905—the year *House of Mirth* was published—Wharton clearly shared at least some part of her friend Teddy's vision of the American "race." Wharton's relationship with the President not only "rested upon belonging to the same social class," as R. W. B. Lewis observes, but the sense of belonging to that social class was nurtured by "reading the same books and enjoying the same jokes."[42] The accident of birth was assiduously maintained and cultivated; essentialism and social construction worked together, for, in the words of Ruth Frankenburg, "biology continued to underwrite conceptions of identity" during this period.[43]

It's hard to imagine Roosevelt, however, the man Henry James called "a dangerous and ominous jingo,"[44] thrilling as Wharton did at Nietzsche's "power of breaking through conventions" in a letter to her friend Sally Norton. Wharton, in the same letter to Sally Norton, daughter of Charles Eliot Norton, a professor at Harvard and frequent contributor to *The Atlantic Monthly,* extolled the experience as "most exhilarating, & clears the air as our thunderstorms just now do—not!" "I think it salutory," she confides, "now & then, to be made to realize what [Nietzsche] calls 'die Unwerthung aller Werthe,' [The reevaluation of all values] and really get back to a wholesome basis of naked instinct."[45] It would seem that Wharton was not then, or perhaps ever, satisfied with the unquestioned union of essentialism and social construction that defined her social class and world; these notions defied what she here calls "naked instinct."

Wharton's "naked instinct" was that of a "race" writer. She took up the task to "collect, preserve, and analyze the most sublime artifacts" of the race she represented, though she did so with a critical eye.[46] Wharton treated what we would call a "class" as a "race" because the terms of this culture were defined by more than just financial means: manners, along with fortune, were inherited traits.[47] The social creed is as much a part of the legacy as the financial means to support the lifestyle out of which it developed. One needed the two together to be a part of the "high" society Wharton saw deteriorating before her eyes. *The House of Mirth* chronicles that deterioration through the events that befall the character Lily Bart. While Lily is nominally part of the upper-echelon social set that she mixes with, she lacks the accompanying fortune to attract a suitable husband. As the novel unfolds, the inescapable need to bankroll her beauty puts Lily in compromising circumstances of mounting seriousness. Unless Lily can "improve" herself through marriage (as all women of this class and period had to) she will deteriorate entirely. Lily's lack of funds—not a lack of character, family background, upbringing, or beauty—brings the novel to a crisis. Her predicament is decisively a sign of the times and Wharton sacrifices one of her most beloved characters to those times in order to criticize the way of life that created such circumstances.

Wharton's dual purpose as race writer—to record and criticize—materializes in the choice of satire for her narrative mode. Satire is the mode of the conservative moralizer who lampoons the tribe only to save and venerate it. In fact, a reviewer of the novel for *The Independent* considered it a call for reform to "the most corrupt class of people in the world."[48] *The House of Mirth,* a study of the class lines that inscribe the terms of Lily's possible marriage matches, satirizes the social codes keeping Lily vulnerable—even though such codes were supposed to protect her. In an opening scene of the novel, Lily grapples with one of the novel's central questions about the nature of difference in gender expectations in class terms: "Who wants a dingy woman?" In a devastating critique of the system, Lily remarks, "Your coat's a little shabby—but who cares? If I were shabby no one would have me: a woman is asked out as much for her clothes as for herself."[49] Wharton explained that the novel achieves tragic status through just this sense of irony; the society inevitably must "waste" its best character, Lily Bart, in order to be what it is: a frivolous society whose only significance lies in "its power of debasing people and ideals."[50] Wharton opposed the changes that were taking place in American society, though she recognized their inevitability in her portrayal of the events that befall Lily Bart—a testament, in other words, to her greatness as an artist rather than a political radical or social activist.[51]

What we must understand in order to understand Wharton's use of race is that she simply read her own culture through the racial and what we would call *racist* lens of her own time. Her novels probe racial issues—sometimes even blatantly through the use of such topics as eugenics and euthanasia—though never to the effect that would assuage our current political consciousness.[52] Thus, calling Edith Wharton a "race" writer is not claiming a metaliberal imagination for Edith Wharton as a person. As Wharton herself says, "There could be no greater critical ineptitude than to judge a novel according to what it ought to have been about."[53] Accordingly, it would be a mistake to claim that Wharton consciously undertook to represent the class of people who make up her subject by portraying them as a race.

III. Race, Realism, and the Marketplace

A close look at lines uttered by Wharton's protagonist in *The House of Mirth* will help us figure out the function of race in Wharton's bestselling 1905 novel: "Why, the beginning was in my cradle, I suppose—in the way I was brought up, and the things I was taught to care for. Or no, I won't blame anybody for my faults: I'll say it was in my blood."[54] These words signal the terms Wharton will use to explore her character's history.[55] Torn between essentialism and social construction, Lily Bart cannot decide if her problems are simply in her "blood" or if her fate is determined by the way she was "brought up." Interestingly, by putting both of these options into play, Wharton offers us a fresh opportunity to consider the function of each in describing the two poles around which theories of race, then and now, have been located. But my interest in the presence of race as an important feature of identity—and the way such considerations lend an element of crisis to the progress of the novel's protagonist—has more to do with how such an emphasis connects Wharton with the literary tradition of realism as I see it unfolding in the United States. Wharton's fidelity to the details of the daily life in turn-of-the-century "old" New York has encouraged contemporary critics to view the novel through anthropological and ethnographical lenses.[56] For good reason and excellent effect, even more recently, Wharton scholars have been focused on establishing race as a feature of identity in Wharton's work. Thus, no matter what voltage critics assign to Wharton's use of race, it is now seen as an uncontested feature of her work. What I'd like to argue for here is the importance of race as an open-ended trope—"the ultimate trope of difference" as Henry Louis Gates, Jr. has termed it—calibrated to interest potential readers. In Wharton's narratives, in other words, it's important that we recognize that race serves as the novel's central (and unsolvable) mystery.[57]

What we can see now is that the tension between essentialism and social construction allows for a multiplicity of views not limited to readers of one class or ideological position, granting the novel a degree of elasticity not shared by its author. Like writers of her period and before, Wharton turned this tension into a narrative mechanism, a way to tell the story of Lily Bart and the many other characters that form the focus of her fiction. Wharton's use of the racial topoi might best be seen as a reflection of her canny sense of the literary standards commanding the marketplace. Coding aristocratic characters in a realist key, new uses of race and class converge in Wharton's novels.

In keeping with racial theories that Wharton was familiar with, this story of the terms of Lily Bart's demise simultaneously describes the basis of Wharton's critique of old New York's racial suicide.[58] Percy Gryce, for instance, Lily's most promising prospect from the old order, best represents the kind of evolutionary stagnation that Wharton saw as responsible for the degeneration of the race. The custodian of an important collection of Americana, Gryce, the narrator observes with a sneer, "took as much pride in his inheritance as though it had been his own(work)."[59] His "personal complacency" stands for the kind of cultural hubris that Wharton not only abhorred but saw as the cause of "high" society's downfall. Rather than work to establish his own place within tradition, "he came to regard himself as figuring prominently in the public eye, and to enjoy the thought of the interest which would be excited if the persons he met in the street, or sat among travelling, were suddenly to be told that he was the possessor of the Gryce Americana."[60] Gryce mistakenly thinks ownership is the same thing as an identity and that possessions will maintain his place (and his race) in history. Provocatively, and in a move that betrays Wharton's ambivalent position both as member and critic of the culture she describes, (that is, as a race writer), Gryce is linked to Nettie Struthers in that they are the only characters in the novel who will reproduce during its course.

Wharton's use of Gryce allows us to examine another important node vibrating with meaning in realist writings; money serves as an index for complex emotional circumstances in all of the works under consideration in this book. Wharton makes use of this convention despite her upper-class subject, or perhaps because of it. The novel outfits itself with the language of commerce and thus connects with "the crowd mentality" of popular taste.[61] Lily's mother is praised by friends for being a "wonderful manager" in her marriage. In the world this novel describes, marriage is likened to a partnership and many of Lily's hardships are treated on a cost-analysis basis. Although these characters may be aristocratic and "high born," they are not above financial worries. In fact, the novel often dwells on the financial feasibility or extravagance of social situations. The inclusion of monetary details almost guarantees reader identification with Lily. What reader doesn't shudder when Lily discovers she's lost a whopping $300 at bridge, gasp when Gus Trenor calls in his debts, and blanch as Lily writes that final check? Money has a real impact on these characters just as it does on real people. By using money as a tangible measure of character suffering and success, this novel of manners succeeded as a popular work of realism. Lily's lack of funds—not a lack of character, family background, upbringing, or beauty—brings the novel to a crisis.

Strategies such as this one enabled *The House of Mirth* to captivate the imagination of many who were well outside Wharton's class, as evidenced by the plethora of mail she received from readers of the novel during its serialization and subsequent popularity. Remarking the poor style and grammatical errors that characterized the admiring mail from readers Wharton would view as from a lower class, she nonetheless kept a trunk full of these "funny" letters.[62] She clearly enjoyed the adulation of the "masses" and delighted in the success of the novel, even if its popularity signified changes in the world she cherished. Edward L. Burlingame, who published her first poem in *Scribner's* in 1889, interpreted *The House of Mirth*'s popularity as a sign of American cultural development. Obviously, the success of the novel registered the paying interest of the less-cultivated reader. Wharton only tentatively agreed with him that "its large circulation is a sign of awakening taste in our fellow countrymen," chastening his assertion with the qualification, "at least 100,000 of them."[63] In part a matter of modesty, Wharton's reluctance to take credit for "uplifting" the standards of American taste also evidences concern for the changes in

American society upon which her success depended. And this brings me to my next focus: the importance of the marketplace on Wharton's literary production.

Wharton was ever vigilant about maximizing the monetary profit on her work; her business acumen was behind schemes to raise money and to open up publishing opportunities for her friend Henry James more than once. Letters to her publishers reveal her "hands-on" approach to the publication and advertising campaigns of her writings. Her involvement in the publication process shows that Wharton was unashamed to make business and financial matters a central concern, which others of her class disdained to do. Upon receipt of her first published novel, Wharton probably surprised her publisher with this reaction to the book's title page: "Words fail to express how completely I don't like it."[64] True to her identity as a consummate woman of action, the remainder of Wharton's letter outlines various problems with the graphics. To Wharton's mind, the workmanship of the actual volume is as much her business as was the writing: "The 'make-up' of the book seems," in Wharton's opinion, "as inappropriate for the style of the story as for its length."[65] Wharton's complaint is not only an aesthetic one; she cannily adds the suggestion that the price of the volume be reduced. Given the botched packaging, "would it not be possible," Wharton wonders, "by way of mending matters, to sell the book for a little less than $2? If it would be sold for $1.75 it seems to me that it would make all the difference."[66] Her concern for the presentation of the book clearly has to do with its marketability and the profits it might turn. The modesty with which she characteristically accepts praise compared to the aggressive and ever-vigilant approach to financial issues suggests that fortune came before fame for Wharton. Money did matter.

The novel's change of title from "A Moment's Ornament" to *The House of Mirth* underscores Wharton's intention to broaden the novel's appeal. The novel's original title emphasized the individual character Lily Bart. Her decision to alter the focus through the change in title resonates with her views on the relationship between situation and character in literature. She doubted that "fiction can be usefully divided into novels of situation and character, since a novel if worth anything at all, is always both, in inextricable combination."[67] In Wharton's mind, the truly successful novel examines the inscription of situation on character and the ways character can be recognized through situation. Coincidentally, we can translate this vision of fiction's elements as a subtle intertwining of what we would call social construction and essentialism. Character, it would seem, is an in-born trait, while situation, because it is entirely relational, is all social construction. Thus her use of the interdependence of character and situation is also a way to preserve the tension race supplies throughout the course of the novel.

Instead of "A Moment's Ornament," then, Wharton took a phrase drawn from Ecclesiastes 7:4 for her title: "The heart of the wise is in the house of mourning; but the heart of fools is in the house of mirth." In full, the cautionary message of the reference suggests the failure of the race to preserve itself and survive its traditions. The publisher's inclusion of the entire reference, however, annoyed Wharton. She argued with some sarcasm that including the whole quotation was heavy-handed and didactic ("I might surely be suspected of plagiarizing from Mrs. Margaret Sangster's beautiful volume, 'Five Days with God,'" Wharton quipped) because the text "inculcates a moral."[68] Clearly, she wanted to retain a level of ambiguity that the full quotation squashes.

Evoking the pity of lower-class readers who sympathize with Lily's plight—to marry in order to preserve her status—and the anxiety in upper-class readers over their own position, Wharton captures the interest of a whole range of readers. The novel motivates a powerful mélange of anger and awe in part through its depiction of the social code and its effects and thus extends the range of responses realism can invoke in readers. Character and situation threaten Lily Bart with extinction for infractions of the social code, infractions that the reader knows are as narratively inevitable as they are socially lamentable. The whole novel has been building up to this betrayal; its justification lies in the nature of Lily Bart's character itself. On some level, the novel seems to suggest, her fate *is* in her blood. She inherited a taste for poetry—through a "vein of sentiment" derived from her father—that led to what readers must construe as a dangerous liking for sentimental fiction. It is this quality that prompts Lily to add an "idealizing touch to her most prosaic purposes," and thus to lose sight of her real circumstances. [69] When she expresses a longing "to drop out of the race and make an independent life for herself," readers—then and now—interpret that desire in two ways. And the central pivot for either interpretation is in the word, "race."

As a critic of American culture, Edith Wharton is also a race writer. Her novels, and this one in particular, turn on the kind of cultural code switching that often formulates the most crucial aspects of identity in what is usually considered race writing. By tracing Lily's unsuccessful translation from slave to mistress, Wharton tells Lily's story in a dialect of being that none of the novel's co-characters can understand. Lily's choices are not a mere mimicry of the social order but a "force of revelation," in Gates's terms, that inflects her experience and the expression of it.[70] The unaccomplished search for the "word" that cannot be spoken by either Lawrence Selden or Lily Bart at the close of this novel exemplifies the need for a new language that can signify—in our critical parlance—an identity, a mode of being, not one that is defined by an ideology of race legislating sameness, but one that accommodates difference.

No matter which construction of race a reader opts for, the force of Lily's wish to somehow get outside the system is what helps to explain our continued identification with her victimization on the basis of this repressive social code. But perhaps more significantly, we continue to identify with Lily Bart despite our own critical evaluations of the privileges of class. We do not put the novel aside as a useless relic, partly because Lily's predicament has more to do with class as a race signifier than with race as a class signifier. For Wharton and members of the society she chronicles, biology—insofar as it represents genealogy—was destiny. Here Wharton's beliefs run against that tradition of realism that holds class as entirely circumstantial; we as a society deeply influenced by this genre have rejected the notion that class is in-born. Yet, as is the case with many great artists, however, Wharton was able to leave the door open to this central ambiguity and thus keep it real.

Epilogue

Keeping it Real

Truth More Marketable than Fiction?

This book has resurrected a literary history that takes the popularity of slave narratives seriously, tracing their transformative power on the literary marketplace of the nineteenth century. As we have seen, the widespread development of print culture dovetailed with the country's need to address the issue of slavery. When William Lloyd Garrison militated for abolition in the pages of *The Liberator,* a new use for "truth" came to the fore. Through the publication of first-hand reports of slavery in the form of slave narratives, Garrison and others fostered an interest in what we've been discussing as "the humanitarian narrative," the use of the description of physical suffering as a means to encourage social justice.[1] Quickly, authors as diverse in style and biography as William Wells Brown, Herman Melville, and Harriet Beecher Stowe all took advantage of this impact of abolition on the fashioning of evangelical readers' tastes, publishing works that presented slavery and the suffering it caused as central to their narratives.

With the remarkable success of slave narratives and works developing their themes, authors and publishers realized that they could parlay writing into income only through a careful consideration of market conditions and that abolition was at the heart of the publishing industry. Centered in New England, publishing venues such as *The Atlantic Monthly* were saturated with the spirit of abolition and thus promoted literary efforts in favor of the cause. Rose Terry Cooke's career is a case in point. Cooke's writings were published widely and she held a prominent place in the pantheon of mid-nineteenth-century writers. Admired by James Russell

Lowell, Mary Wilkins Freeman, William Dean Howells, and Sarah Orne Jewett for her realist treatment and fiery viewpoints on gender and New England culture, Cooke's writing enjoyed a wide readership, one informed by the humanitarian ethos of the era.

But Reconstruction politics had as deep an impact on literary tastes as did the abolitionist movement of the earlier period. Born of authors' needs to make a living and to respond to the humanitarian impulse at the core of a white, middle-class readership, realism took shape in what historian David Blight has described as a climate of increasing racial renunciation.[2] Postbellum fiction readers' tastes demonstrated less and less the need to address and change the status of African Americans in the United States. Rather than take on the problems that would only continue to fester from Reconstruction on, readers restricted their humanitarian interests to their own class and race issues.[3] It is at this moment in the literary development of the United States that the genealogy of the slave narratives was written out of literary history. As we saw in the review of contracts between realist writer William Dean Howells and his publishers, readers called for works that focused on "average" American characters. In late-nineteenth-century America, the average American was white.

By 1905, Edith Wharton's *House of Mirth* shared space on the *Publisher's Weekly* fiction bestseller list with Thomas Dixon, Jr.'s racist classic, *The Clansman.*[4] Dixon's novel ranked fourth while Wharton's book was in eighth place. And there were other ways in which the popularity of Dixon's book exceeded that of Wharton's novel. The novel was transformed into a blockbusting movie by D. W. Griffith in 1915. Griffith's *The Birth of the Nation* remains important for its innovative motion picture techniques, most notably those used to depict the assassination of Abraham Lincoln. Wharton's book, on the other hand, though also made into a film, failed critically as well as historically: the original print is now lost.[5] The relative popularity of these two texts makes plain that the relationship between literature and social structure can be interpreted (and not merely interpolated) through the marketplace.

We might turn to the work of African American journalist and social activist, Ida B. Wells to help us understand the meaning of the popularity of works that adopt a white (racist) point of view. Born a slave in 1862, Wells was the first to attribute violent racism to a form of class anxiety in her book, *Southern Horrors: Lynch Law in all its Phases* (1892).[6] There and elsewhere, she maintained that lynching was a means for keeping blacks down economically by eliminating those who prospered. The popularity of *The Clansman* and the film *Birth of a Nation,* which was based on it, offers compelling evidence of Wells's thesis as well as of the racist disposition of the book-buying public of the time.

And the same racist logic still seems to hold. Even after World War II magnified the erasure of these works, African American writers have been notably absent. Not until 1946, with the career of Frank Yerby, did a black writer grace such a list.[7] And then it was over 50 years before another such author—Toni Morrison—would once again appear on the *Publishers' Weekly* fiction bestseller list.[8] Meanwhile, in addition to Edith Wharton, white authors such as Willa Cather, William Faulkner, Ernest Hemingway, Sinclair Lewis, and John Steinbeck all appeared repeatedly on the bestseller lists.[9] As a group, these novelists take social justice as their theme. No matter how different their settings and styles may be from each other, they can all be considered descendents of the humanitarian realists as they have been defined here. Thus, it was not social relevance that was unpopular with readers; rather class concerns came to replace the humanitarian interest in race of the earlier era. Clearly the subject of racial equality had become not just unpopular but "unimaginable," in Philip Fisher's terms, in a post-Reconstructionist era.[10]

Aside from Frank Yerby, African American writers such as Richard Wright in 1945 and Alex Haley in 1976, only appeared on the non-fiction list. Despite the publishing phenomenon we know as the Harlem Renaissance, none of the works that appeared during that time are listed as bestsellers on the *Publishers' Weekly* list. Nor were any of the classic African American works such as Ralph Ellison's *Invisible Man* (which won the National Book Award in 1953) or Alice Walker's Pulitzer Prize–winning *The Color Purple* (1982). Though the list has been increasingly dominated by mass-market, pulp fiction and genre novels such as those by Judith Krantz or James Michener, there has always been room on the fiction list for writers such as J. D. Salinger, William Styron, Saul Bellow and a bevy of other white writers.

The erasure of race in favor of class issues continues in our own time. Today, memoir is among the bestselling genres in the literary marketplace. Drawing much of the humanitarian interest in their stories from the hardships of poverty rather than racial inequalities, these modern-day memoirists awaken in their readers a sense of privilege and comfort. Written for a white middle-class readership lacking the reform spirit of an earlier era, today's memoirs take their writers on a familiar trail of promotional stops. They go on book tours and talk radio and television shows; the publishers place ads in newspapers and magazines; and the publicists urge journalists to write about the authors.

In many ways, today's memoirists follow the leads of earlier realists: in making their stories heart-wrenchingly real, they capture a readership that exceeds their immediate demographic. You don't have to be Irish—or even an immigrant—to feel Frank McCourt's story, nor do you have to be from East Texas and have a psychotic mother to empathize with Mary Karr. However, unlike their predecessors, these texts do not carry with them an explicit social agenda. Beautifully written and exquisitely told, these are stories about the resilience of the human spirit, not the flaws of our social system. They are not bitter nor do they offer a critique of the social structures that gave rise to many of the circumstances that they relate. Why do these books lack the zeal for social justice epitomized by humanitarian realism? Part of the reason must be that writers have learned the lesson that literary history has taught us: Capitalize on the preexisting generic styles in order to increase sales. I suppose it is up to us, as readers, critics and literary historians, to keep it real.

Indeed, we might say that we have come to a new plateau regarding race as an appropriate feature for fiction in the twenty-first century. This week, 22 July 2001, five novels by and about African Americans are on the *New York Times* bestseller list. We might read the success of these books as signs of change in the literary marketplace. Commenting on this historic moment, Henry Louis Gates, Jr., remarked, "This reflects the new capacity of the broader American public to identify with black characters . . . Fifty years ago, white readers read Richard Wright to learn about the Other; now many whites have the capacity to see themselves through a black character."[11] Sanguine words, to be sure. Dare we hope that they represent a new truth—one that is stranger and stronger than fiction?

Notes

Introduction

1. For a perfect illustration of how these factors converged, consider the American Tract Society. It was the first—and most profitable—company to take advantage of the innovations of the printing press, using technological advances to foster a readership that would buy its publications.
2. Thomas H. Gossett, in *Race: The History of an Idea* (New York: Oxford, 1997), traces the impact of racism on the development of American literary history, focusing, in particular, on the importance of Anglo-Saxon language and literature in English Departments as an effort to legitimize American literature as descended from the same race (128–143). Toni Morrison, in *Playing in the Dark: Whiteness and the Literary Imagination* (New York: Vintage, 1993) explores the repression of African American influences in U.S. literary history from a more literary point of view.
3. Earlier critics may have "hailed realistic characterization and plot as a necessary adjunct to the acceptance of black Americans as full participants in American society" as Kenneth Warren notes in *Black and White Strangers: Race and American Literary Realism* (Chicago: U of Chicago P, 1993), yet they have failed to see the specifically American context for what has typically been thought of as a French import (4).
4. "Correspondence between the Hon. F. H. Elmore and James G. Birney," *The Anti-Slavery Examiner* (New York: American Anti-Slavery Society, 1838), 19–20, quoted in Ann Fabian, *The Unvarnished Truth: Personal Narratives in Nineteenth-Century America* (Berkeley: U of California P, 2000), 80.
5. Michael Davitt Bell, *The Problem of American Realism: Studies in the Cultural History of an Idea.* Chicago: U of Chicago, P., 1993, 1. Indeed, for many critics, realism's lack of a coherent aesthetic has been a source for valuing its richness. Michael Anesko sums up this position thus: "The failure of coherence . . . is less a liability than a source of interest, because it reveals the peculiar instability of realism's aesthetic and social functions and the multiple ways in which that instability can be registered and analyzed." Michael Anesko, "Recent Critical Approaches," in *The Cambridge Companion to American Realism and Naturalism.* ed. Donald Pizer (Cambridge: Cambridge UP, 1995), 82.

6. "Bodies, Details, and the Humanitarian Narrative," *The New Cultural History,* ed. Lynn Hunt (Berkeley: U of California P, 1989), 176–205. Thomas Laqueur links the social history of eighteenth-century British humanitarianism to the proliferation and variation of narrative texts that rely on the body to prompt social action. See also, E. Clark, "'The Sacred Rights of the Weak': Pain, Sympathy, and the Culture of Individual Rights in Antebellum America," *Journal of American History* 82 (September 1995): 463–93.
7. Though I will be discussing an earlier era of realism in relation to African American literature and culture, I am indebted to Kenneth Warren's *Black and White Strangers* and in particular to his suggestion that we "must try to account for the strong belief in the emancipatory powers of realism by looking at the effects of those beliefs within and without literary texts" (9).
8. Many critics of American realism simply consider it a French import. See, for instance, Werner Berthoff (*The Ferment of Realism: American Literature, 1884–1919* [New York: Free Press, 1965]) and Alfred Kazin (*On Native Grounds: An Interpretation of American Prose Literature* [Garden City, NY: Doubleday, 1956]). These are two critics, among others, who have thought of American realism as "a borrowed label" (in Berthoff's words) rather than an authentic movement as it is said to be in France.
9. In 1921, *The Age of Innocence* was on the Publisher's Weekly bestseller list; it also won the Pulitzer Prize. Six years later, Wharton's *Twilight Sleep* appeared on the bestseller list.

Chapter 1

1. This chapter results from the care of many. My thanks to Jan Cooper, Robert Fanuzzi, Laura May Grayson, Robert Iltis, Amy Kaplan, Wendy Kozol, Henry Mayer, Whitney Pape, Paula Richman, Priscilla Wald, and Sandy Zagarell for their thoughtful responses, suggestions, encouragement, and overall good friendship. This study has also benefited from the generosity (both financial and librarian) of Mudd Library, Oberlin College and the Library Company of Philadephia. Special thanks to anonymous readers from *American Literature:* your reviews helped strengthen the essay version of this chapter in significant ways; and to Houston Baker for seeing it through.
2. Prefatory poem in *Words of Garrison* (Boston: Houghton, Mifflin and Co., 1905).
3. Both William Andrews, *To Tell a Free Story* (Urbana: U of Illinois P, 1986) and Frances Smith Foster *Witnessing Slavery* (Madison: U of Wisconsin P, 1994, 2nd ed.) discuss Garrison's role in proliferating slave narratives through his press and the pages of *The Liberator.* Charles Sellers, *The Market Revolution* (New York: Oxford, 1991) credits Garrison with actually originating the use of slave narratives for the abolitionist cause noting that his followers were "radicalized by the novel white experience of listening to what blacks were saying" in the pages of *The Liberator* (402). Thus, Gar-

rison came to see "southern slavery's brutality as epitomizing the national sin of racism" (402).

4. Sellers, *The Market Revolution,* 405.
5. For a discussion of Garrison's political philosophy as developing along side of innovations in print media, see Robert Fanuzzi's "The Organ of an Individual: William Lloyd Garrison and The *Liberator,*" *Prospects* (1998): 107–27. Here I concur with him in the merits of looking closely at *The Liberator;* in his view, the study of *The Liberator* offers us "the opportunity to see how a historically conscious reform movement adapted these republican ideals not only to the uncongenial circumstances of the Jacksonian era but to the identity of a single person" (109). In what follows, I expand that appreciation to consider *The Liberator* as a galvanizing force in the literary marketplace.
6. As Charles Sellers has observed, "Abolition burgeoned especially among people trying, like Garrison, to reconcile self-making egotism with ancestral altruism through the intense Christian piety of Finneyite benevolence." See *The Market Revolution,* 404. Robert Abzug, in *Cosmos Crumbling: American Reform and the Religious Imagination* (New York: Oxford, 1994), puts a finer point on Sellers' assessment: "Alienated from the web of social and church order, radical reformers [such as Garrison] sought to make American society holy by broadening and sacralizing the meaning of equality, by making sacred the details of everyday life, and by reimagining the basic structure of society on earth and spiritual being after death . . .[challenging] some of the most basic American assumptions concerning the individual, society, and cosmos: white racial superiority, marriage, prevailing dietary and medical practice, individualistic values of the marketplace, the centrality of the church to religious life, and the nature of death" (127).
7. John L. Thomas, *The Liberator: William Lloyd Garrison* (Boston: Little, Brown, 1963), 21.
8. James Brewer Stewart, *William Lloyd Garrison and the Challenge of Emancipation* (Arlington Heights, IL: Harian Davidson, Inc, 1992), 14.
9. The late Henry Mayer, in the most recent biography of Garrison, *All on Fire* (New York: St. Martin's, 1998), views Garrison's efforts to ignite interest in abolition as countercultural. Linking his idealism to the depth of his commitment to the cause, Mayer's evaluation is particularly useful to this discussion as it reinvigorates Garrison as an iconoclast.
10. That abolitionism emerged into an ever-widening marketplace is suggested by the increase in groups and services devoted to the cause. According to Frank Luther Mott, "the number of local societies in the [antislavery] movement increased from one hundred in 1926 to two thousand by 1840, with over 175,000 members." See *A History of American Magazines,* 5 vols. (Cambridge: Harvard UP, 1967), vol. I, 456. The development of a market to serve these tastes beckoned Garrison, a natural-born entrepreneur. In addition to Robert Fanuzzi's article, see David

Paul Nord's essay, "Toqueville, Garrison and the Perfection of Journalism," *Journalism History* 13:2 (Summer 1986), 56–64, for an examination of Garrison's professionalization of abolition through journalism.

11. Stewart, *William Lloyd Garrison and the Challenge of Emancipation,* 106.
12. I have used the four black abolitionist newspapers indexed in Donald M. Jacobs' *Antebellum Black Newspapers: Indices to Freedom's Journal (1827–1829), The Rights of All (1829), The Weekly Advocate (1837) and The Colored American (1837–1841)* (Westport, CT: Greenwood, 1976) as my sample.
13. Fanuzzi, "The Organ of an Individual," 111–12.
14. *The Colored American,* 16 February 1829, quoted in Jacobs, *Antebellum Black Newspapers,* 287.
15. As Ann Fabian observes, "some [former slaves] used accounts of storytelling to denounce their old gifts for the lie, marking the moral distance they had traveled from slavery." *The Unvarnished Truth,* 102.
16. According to historians John Blassingame and Mae Henderson, editors of the five-volume, annotated list of letters to the editors from abolitionist papers, the "combined circulation figure (for abolition papers) was higher than that of such better known contemporaries as the *New York Times* in the nineteenth-century." See *Antislavery Newspapers and Periodicals,* edited by John W. Blassingame and Mae G. Henderson (Boston: G. K. Hall, 1980–1984), Vol. II, xi. So, although alternative papers did not really provide competition to the major dailies (see Edwin C. Baker, *Advertising and a Democratic Press,* [Princeton UP, 1994], 36), they circulated widely to an ever-increasing niche market. These papers freely reprinted articles and letters from other publications, and crediting the source was part of the piece's attraction. Just as the penny press came to report the mode by which information was received—news by telegraph, for instance, was far more attractive than news by pony express—these papers introduced reprinted stories by way of their published sources. This practice created a kind of network in which people who read one paper, in effect, read many papers in regard to this subject.
17. Thomas, *The Liberator,* 131.
18. Thomas, *The Liberator,* 132.
19. On the history of advertising in the United States, see Frank Presbrey, *The History and Development of Advertising* (New York: Doubleday, 1929) and the more recent Jackson Lears, *Fables Of Abundance: A Cultural History of Advertising in America* (New York: Basic Book, 1994).
20. Nord explores the link between Garrison's perfectionism and the rise of U.S. journalism in "Tocqueville, Garrison and the Perfection of Journalism."
21. *The Liberator,* 1 January 1833, 1. The passage printed here maintains the various type fluctuations as they appear in the original *Liberator,* William Lloyd Garrison, ed., Boston: 1831–1865.
22. See figure 1.1 for an example of 5 1/2 point agate type that was standard. Throughout the rest of this article, scanned images from the actual *Libera-*

tor are used as illustrations. The phrase is from Fanuzzi, "The Organ of an Individual," 109.

23. In this respect, Garrison was following in the footsteps of his English counterparts, abolitionists such as Thomas Clarkson and William Wilberforce. But Garrison and his fellow American abolitionists managed to circulate their message much more broadly thanks to the transportation and communication revolution in the United States. Nord, "Tocqueville, Garrison and the Perfection of Journalism," 56–63. See also, Thomas, *The Liberator,* 120–23; Presbrey, *The History and Development of Advertising,* 226.
24. Thomas W. Laqueur, "Bodies, Details, and the Humanitarian Narrative," in *The New Cultural History,* ed. Lynn Hunt (Berkeley: U of California P, 1989), 176–205.
25. Stewart, *William Lloyd Garrison and the Challenge of Emancipation,* 14.
26. We can trace Garrison's creativity with typeface and layout to his involvement with Benjamin Lundy's *Genius of Universal Emancipation.* Garrison served as an assistant editor to Lundy for six months in 1829 and while in that position radicalized both the form and content of the paper. Upon his departure in 1830 the paper was restored to its original look.
27. For instance, the first advertisements—both nationally and internationally—were notices of runaway slaves. See Presbrey, *The History and Development of Advertising,* and Raymond Williams, "Advertising: The Magic System," *Problems in Materialism and Culture,* (New York: Schocken Books, 1980), 170–196.
28. Baker, *Advertising and a Democratic Press,* 6–15; Michael Schudson, *Discovering the News: A Social History of American Newspapers,* (New York: Basic: 1978), 66.
29. Mott, *A History of American Magazines.*
30. Presbrey, *The History and Development of Advertising,* 232.
31. As a point of comparison: *The National Era* announced availability of advertising space in the section where the ads themselves appeared during this period.
32. In a similar fashion, products developed in response to the success of *Uncle Tom's Cabin.* Songs, board games, crockery and other paraphernalia were developed to take advantage of the novel's popularity. For a full discussion of the ephemera generated by *Uncle Tom's Cabin,* see Marcus Wood, *Blind Memory: Visual Representations of Slavery in England and America, 1780–1865* (New York: Routledge, 2000), 143–215.
33. Mott, *A History of American Magazines,* vol. II, 281.
34. Williams, "Advertising: The Magic System," 170.
35. Thomas, *The Liberator,* 119.
36. Garrison split from other abolitionists over the issue of Woman's Rights. Under his leadership, the American Anti-Slavery Society encouraged women in leadership roles.
37. Many ads were geared for a female audience, selling products in the vanity market that traditionally has been considered the purview of woman, as well as other health and family products—another stronghold of female

influence. As Karen Sanchez-Eppler points out in *Touching Liberty: Abolition, Feminism, and the Politics of the Body* (Berkeley and Los Angeles: U of California P, 1993), Garrison made clear the importance of women to the abolitionist movement by including a section called "The Ladies Department" as a regular feature in *The Liberator* (23).

38. Fabian, *The Unvarnished Truth,* 80.
39. This seeming harmony was short-lived, however. By the end of the 19th century, capital cannot be separated from the operations of a secular, consumer culture—the kind famously condemned by Thorstein Veblen's bold *Theory of a Leisure Class* (1899). For a discussion of the shortcomings of Veblen's theory, especially as it pertains to the earlier era that I focus on in the first three chapters of this book, see Jackson Lears, "Beyond Veblen: Rethinking Consumer Culture in America," in *Consuming Visions: Accumulation and Display of Goods in America, 1880–1920,* ed. Simon J. Bronner (New York: Norton, 1989).
40. Benedict Anderson, *Imagined Communities: Reflections on the Origin and the Spread of Nationalism* (London; New York: Verso, 1983) 14–15.
41. Thanks to Robert Fanuzzi for refining this point for me.
42. A "Requited Labor Grocery and Labor Store," run by Lydia White, was the sole purveyor for the Mott household, for instance, because upon an examination of her conscience, Lucretia Mott felt it was "her duty to boycott all products made by slave labor." Thomas, *The Liberator,* 118–90. Hicksite Quakers, Lucretia and James Mott were great supporters of Garrison and were also part of "a transatlantic community of Quakers in England and the United States that thrived on trade, manufacturing, and the multiplication of investments." Stewart, *William Lloyd Garrison and the Challenge of Emancipation,* 49. They were both commercially adept and morally correct.
43. *The Liberator,* 30 April 1856, 97; 27 July 1855, 119; 5 August 1853, 122.
44. In fact, Barnum used this form of advertising to get attention for his first "freak" exhibit—a supposed 161-year-old former slave of George Washington's named Joice Heth. See Presbrey, *The History and Development of Advertising,* 213–14.
45. In *Touching Liberty,* Karen Sanchez-Eppler describes the effectiveness of rhetorical use of the body by both abolitionists and feminists as achieved in part through "moments of identification." In this process the body of an otherwise unassimilatable "other" is unconsciously assimilated through the description of shared experiences of physical and emotional suffering. See especially 14–49.
46. *The Liberator,* 2 December 1853, 191.
47. *The Liberator,* 25 January 1856, 16.
48. *The Liberator,* 18 June 1852, 98; 12 September 1851, 148.
49. *The Liberator,* 23 December 1853, 203
50. Mott, *A History of American Magazines,* vol. II, 131.
51. See Russel Nye, *Fettered Freedom: Civil Liberties and the Slavery Controversy* (East Lansing: Michigan State College Press, 1949) for discussion of this topic.

52. The superintendent of the eighth census in 1862 reports the rise in political papers was almost 100 percent from 1,630 in 1850 to 3,242 in 1860. See Mott, *A History of American Magazines,* vol. II, 131.
53. For this analysis, I counted only the first appearance of an advertised product, not the number of times it appears during the year, because ad space was often purchased on an annual basis.
54. See Sanchez-Eppler for further remarks on the salable quality of abolitionist works, *Touching Liberty: Abolition, Feminism, and the Politics of the Body,* 24–25.
55. *The National Era* did not grant advertisers the same privileges. Books were sold through mention of title, publishers, price, and, sometimes, author; their ideological tie-in with abolition was never mentioned.
56. Readers of this chapter will recall the article against fiction that appeared in *The Colored American* discussed earlier.
57. Sanchez-Eppler, *Touching Liberty: Abolition, Feminism, and the Politics of the Body,* 20.
58. *The Liberator,* 1 January 1833, 1.
59. Thomas W. Laqueur, "Bodies, Details, and the Humanitarian Narrative." See also, Elizabeth B. Clark's "'The Sacred Rights of the Weak': Pain, Sympathy, and the Culture of Individual Rights in Antebellum America" (*The Journal of American History* :82[September 1995]: 463–93) for a discussion of how the image of the suffering slave played "a crucial role in an unfolding language of individual rights" (463).
60. The phrase is taken from Charles T. Davis, and Henry Louis Gates, Jr., *The Slave's Narrative.* (New York: Oxford, 1985), 29. For a discussion of the construction of "artlessness" as a socially conditioned category filled with racist implications, see Ann Fabian, *The Unvarnished Truth,* 107–12.
61. Davis and Gates, *The Slave's Narrative,* 29.
62. Henry Bibb's *Narrative of the Life and Adventures of Henry Bibb, an American Slave* was published in 1849. Together with Douglass and Josiah Henson, Bibb is among those who set the standards for slave narratives in the antebellum period.
63. Ann Fabian, *The Unvarnished Truth,* 101.
64. Davis and Gates, *The Slave's Narrative,* 30.

Chapter 2

1. The research I present here was made possible by a McLean Contributorship Fellowship awarded by the Library Company of Philadelphia. Thanks to librarians James Green, Ruth Hughes, and Phil Lapansky and visiting fellow Jon Stephen Miller, my stay there was both productive and pleasant. My Radcliffe Junior Research Partner, Avi Steinberg, was indispensable to the development of this chapter, which I wrote while on appointment at the Bunting Fellowship Program, Radcliffe Institute for Advanced Research, Harvard University. My "sister fellows," most notably Alice Jarrard,

Francesca Polletta, Silvia Spitta, and Shellburne Thurber offered critical support throughout my year at the Bunting. As always, I am in awe of the intellectual and personal generosity of friends and colleagues in the field, especially Priscilla Wald who read and commented copiously on this essay at a crucial stage. Her example as a teacher, scholar, and friend is a source of inspiration.

2. Scholarship on the slave narratives is both rich and copious. My study of them has been formed largely by the work of William Andrews, Houston Baker, Mia Bay, Russ Castronovo, Frances Foster, Henry Louis Gates, Jr., Deborah E. McDowell, Arnold Rampersad, Rafia Safir, Robert Stepto, Priscilla Wald, and Marcus Wood. Perhaps most important in this connection, is William Andrews's evaluation of the genre as the only one to have "had a mass impact on the consciousness of antebellum Americans." William Andrews, *To Tell a Free Story* (Urbana: U of Illinois P, 1986), 5.
3. Frances Smith Foster, *Witnessing Slavery* 2nd ed. (Madison: U of Wisconsin P 1994), 3–232.
4. Foster, *Witnessing Slavery,* 22.
5. Many scholars consider this text to be the better book. Most helpful to me in understanding *My Bondage and My Freedom* in terms of Douglass's development as an author is Priscilla Wald's discussion of the book and its reception in *Constituting Americans: Cultural Anxiety and Narrative Form* (Durham: Duke UP, 1995), 73–105.
6. It wasn't until the 1880s, when international copyright law went into effect, thanks to the efforts of authors such as Mark Twain and others, that American writers could count on royalties from foreign publication without doing a lot of fancy footwork. For a detailed analysis and accounts of this complicated history see Grantland S. Rice, *The Transformation of Authorship in America* (Chicago UP, 1997) and Michael Warner's *The Letters of the Republic* (Harvard UP, 1990), as well as Cathy N. Davidson's superb mainstay study of the history of authorship, *Revolution and the Word* (New York: Oxford UP, 1986) and David Hall's *Cultures of Print* (Amherst: U of Massachusetts U, 1995). For a focus on the rise of the professional author as it coincided with an emerging print market, see Ronald Weber's *Hired Pens* (Athens: Ohio UP, 1997) and the collection of essays in *Periodical Literature in Nineteenth Century America* ed. Kenneth Price and Susan Belasco Smith (U of Virginia P, 1995).
7. Records do not exist to document fully Douglass's income or financial situation but we can glean a sense of his financial trajectory from available materials. We know, for instance, that between 1839 and 1845, his income was scant. For instance, when he and Anna moved to Lynn, Massachusetts, the Anti-Slavery Society put together funds toward the down payment for a small house by the railroad tracks. For the first time in his life, Douglass had a steady income; he was an agent for the Anti-Slavery Society. We can assume the pay was low, however, because we also know that Anna and the two other women who shared the household took in piecemeal sewing to

help pay bills. We also know that Douglass encouraged donations to help make ends meet for his household and the three small children they were raising. After the publication of the 1845 *Narrative,* however, finances significantly improved. Between 1845 and 1855, when Douglass published *My Bondage and My Freedom,* he had raised 500 pounds in England, bought his own printing press for *The North Star,* and had begun investing in real estate. He eventually owned two houses in Rochester and two adjacent lots. By the time his house on South Avenue burned down in 1872, Douglass had, in addition to his real assets, 11,000 in bonds. See William S. McFeely, *Frederick Douglass* (New York: Touchstone, 1991) and Maria Diedrich, *Love Across the Color Lines: Ottilie Assing and Frederick Douglass* (New York: Hill and Wang, 1999).

8. Letter dated, 29 January 1846. Cited in Fredrick Douglass, *The Life and Writings of Fredrick Douglass,* ed. Phillip Foner (New York: International Publishers, 1950), 136.
9. Nell Irvin Painter, *Sojourner Truth, A Life, A Symbol* (New York: Norton, 1996), 103.
10. As with many of the works under discussion in this chapter, exact sales figures are not available. I, like so many scholars in the field, use numbered editions and material acquisitions (such as the purchase of family out of slavery, or, as in Truth's case, a house) to gauge income. In Truth's case we are especially handicapped because she choose to publish the book herself and retain the plates so that she could print copies as she needed them. Instead of investing in a full run of an edition, Truth could keep her cash and not have to lug around extra copies. When she needed copies, she simply stopped in at the local printer's office and arranged to have the books made up.
11. Painter, *Sojourner Truth, A Life, A Symbol,* 112.
12. 58 percent to be precise. For this study I have focused on slave narratives published in the United States between 1845 and 1870 in book form. Through I have also examined many narratives published in pamphlet form, I have not made them a focus due to their ephemeral nature. Since this is a study of authorship as well as an analysis of the roots of realism, these limitations seem reasonable.
13. Robert Stepto, *From Behind the Veil: A Study of Afro-American Narrative* (Urbana: U of Illinois P, 1979).
14. Foster, *Witnessing Slavery,* 148.
15. According to John J. McCusker's "How Much is That in Real Money? A Historical Price Index for Use as a Deflator of Money Value in the Economy of the United States," *Proceedings of the American Antiquarian Society* 101, pt. 2 (1992): 297–373, we should use a 1:17 ratio to calculate the inflation rate.
16. Although this is not my concern here, readers may be interested in exploring the relationship between photography and realism. For work on that subject, see Miles Orvell, *The Real Thing: Imitation and Authenticity in American Culture, 1880–1940* (Chapel Hill: U of North Carolina P, 1989);

John Pultz, *The Body and the Lens: Photography 1839 to the Present* (New York: Abrahms, 1995); and Alan Trachtenberg, *Reading American Photographs: Images as History, Mathew Brady to Walker Evans* (New York: Hill and Wang, 1989).

17. Here I am using the terms "emergent" and "dominant" according to the model of culture set out by Raymond Williams in *Marxism and Literature* (New York: Oxford UP: 1977), 122–27.
18. Remember, James Williams did not publish his novel as a novel. Instead he used the popularity of slave narratives to get into print. *Narrative of James Williams, an American slave; who was for several years a driver on a cotton plantation in Alabama* (New York; American Anti-Slavery Society, 1838). Though, for Ann Fabian in *The Unvarnished Truth* (Chicago: U of Chicago P, 2000), the jury is still out as to whether or not Williams's story is true: "For all we know," she writes, "Williams may have be a confidence man, trading on northern interest in stories by fugitives and happy to find the means to put an ocean between himself and his pursuers" (93). Henry Louis Gates, Jr., in a lecture delivered at Harvard on 10 December 1999, made a case for rechristening this work a novel.
19. Karen Sanchez-Eppler notes the inversion of the model of authorship as it applies to slave narrators: "The position of the author gains its privilege, precisely because the text produced occludes the specific body of the person who produced it. Inverting this pattern, slave narratives, and perhaps all confessional or testimonial genres, rhetorically create an authorial body. Rather than attempt to assert the incorporeality of authorship, testimonial writing inscribes the author's bodily existence and experience." *Touching Liberty: Abolition, Feminism, and the Politics of the Body* (Berkeley, Los Angeles: U of California P, 1993) 136.
20. According to Charles Nichols, all of Henson's literary productions generated phenomenal sales. "Josiah Henson's narrative had sold six thousand copies in 1852, having been published in England as well as America. By 1858 advanced orders for the 'Stowe edition' of Henson's book totaled 5,000 copies. In the 1878 edition it is claimed that 100,000 copies of the earlier book had been sold. Henson's life story was translated into Dutch and French." *Many Thousands Gone* (Leiden, Netherlands: E. J. Bill, 1963) xiv-xv.
21. Harriet Beecher Stowe, "Introduction" to Josiah Henson's *Truth Stronger Than Fiction, Father Henson's Story of His Own Life* (Boston: J. P. Jewett, 1858) iii.
22. Stowe, *Truth Stronger Than Fiction,* iv-v.
23. Henson, *Truth Stronger Than Fiction,* 204.
24. Henson, *Truth Stronger Than Fiction,* 185.
25. McCusker, "How Much is That in Real Money?," 297–373.
26. Henry Louis Gates, Jr., *Figures in Black* (New York: Oxford, 1987), 82.
27. Charles Sellers, *The Market Revolution,* (New York: Oxford 1991), 405.
28. The first issue of the *Boston Investigator* appeared on Saturday, 2 April 1831. At $2 per annum, it was comparable to *The Liberator* in price. In its

Prospectus it explored the meaning of the motto posted below the paper's title: *Audi Alteram parte* (hear all sides then decide). The paper claimed interest in the facts without taking any side but the side of "truth." For Kneeland, as the paper makes clear, truth can only be found among those who support a whole range of causes, including the usual ones—abolition, women's rights, as well as the elimination of debtor's laws for those who simply cannot pay—not those who just don't want to pay—and all other aspects that are prejudicial to the working classes. Special thanks to James Green at the Library Company of Philadelphia for bringing the newspaper to my attention.

29. For an in-depth discussion of the ideological differences between the labor movement and Garrisonian abolition, see John Ashworth's *Slavery, Capitalism, and Politics in the Antebellum Republic,* (New York: Cambridge, 1995), 148–74. For consideration of the racist underpinnings of class in the Unites States, see David Roediger, *The Wages of Whiteness: Race and the Making of the American Working Class* (London: Verso, 1991).
30. *A Narrative of the Life of Noah Davis A Colored Man Written by Himself, at the age of fifty-four.* (Baltimore: John F. Weishampel, Jr., 1859). Ann Fabian discusses Davis's "learning the art of the artless performance" demanded by the abolitionist market in *The Unvarnished Truth,* 107.
31. Remembering Brown's success with his narrative, we know that Davis's is therefore comparable at least in terms of sales. Of course, we cannot tell if they were anywhere near as brisk.
32. This figure comes close to what Henson raised prior to publication as discussed in note 31.
33. 1 Timothy 5:8.
34. Harriet Jacobs and Harriet Wilson also fall into the category of authors who wrote with the explicit purposes of financial gain.
35. The first and perhaps best example of a slave narrative that supported its author is *The Interesting Narrative of Olauduah Equiano.* Not only did he support himself through the sales and promotion of his book, but he raised a family through the fruits of authorship. James Green recovered the narrative's publishing history, a feat of historical detective work. Thanks to his work, we know how successful Equiano was and why. As Green points out, "Being an author was a hard, full-time job, but not as hard as being a sailor, his earlier occupation. It also paid better; one of his two daughters inherited £950 on her twenty-first birthday. See the "The Publishing History of Olaudah Equiano's *Interesting Narrative,*" *Slavery & Abolition* Great Britain 16.3 (1995): 366. For a full-length discussion of the personal story as a money-making genre in the nineteenth century, see Ann Fabian, *The Unvarnished Truth.*
36. Indeed, I have found at least two examples—thanks to Richard Newman's working bibliography of African American publications—in which the need to make a living through publication was part of the text's title. See, for instance, Robert Voorhis, *Life and Adventures of Robert Voorhis, the Hermit*

of Massachusetts, Who Has Lived Fourteen Years in a Cave, Secluded from Human Society. Comprising an account of his Birth, Parentage, Sufferings, and Providential Escape from Unjust and Cruel Bondage in Early Life—and His Reasons for Becoming a Recluse. Taken from his own mouth by Henry Trumbell, and published for his Benefit (Providence: for Henry Trumbell, 1829). For an example of a broadside developed and sold in the same manner, see: Mrs. Nancy J. Smith, *To the public. Mrs. Nancy J. Smith, formerly a Slave, in Petersburg, VA., having since lost her eyesight, (by a Cancer) and not wishing to become a burden to the public, takes this means of gaining a livelihood for herself, and most respectfully craves your patronage. The Blind Woman's Appeal* (Broadside, n.p.: n.d. [1850?]).

37. Andrews, *To Tell a Free Story,* n. 29, 301.
38. Abzug, Robert. *Cosmos Crumbling: American Reform and the Religious Imagination* (New York: Oxford, 1994), 127; Charles Sellers, *The Market Revolution* (New York: Oxford, 1991), 404.
39. Thomas H. Jones. *The Experience of Thomas H. Jones, Who Was A Slave For Forty-Three Years* (Boston: Bazin and Chandler, 1862), unnumbered page of "Preface," my emphasis.
40. Ashworth, *Slavery, Capitalism, and Politics in the Antebellum Republic,* 151.
41. Henry Louis Gates, Jr. *Figures in Black,* 82.
42. Foster, *Witnessing Slavery,* 22.
43. Foster, *Witnessing Slavery,* 24.
44. Previously, scholars have compared the popularity of the slave narratives to the works of canonized authors, such as Foster's example discussed here. Such comparisons strike me as "apple to orange" because they use works that were not "popular." My "apple to apple" comparisons feature works that were in the popular marketplace alongside slave narratives.
45. Foster notes the use of titles to suggest the generic conventions of slave narratives in later publications of black writers looking for a market (*Witnessing Slavery,* 92). The examples discussed here extend her insight by recognizing the use of titles as a way to link the texts produced during the height of the slave narrative's popularity.
46. Lee and Shepard (1862–1904) specialized in juvenile literature and also developed a nonfiction list, including among their list of authors Charles Sumner, Horace Mann, Wendell Phillips, and the Reverend Charles Beecher.
47. Baker published 31 novels during the course of her career and served as the editor of *Happy Home and Parlor* magazine from 1855 to 1859.
48. Arna Bontemps, "The Slave Narratives: An American Genre." *Great Slave Narratives* (Boston: Beacon Hill Press, 1869), xviii.
49. Lippincott continued to show a flair for controversial works, publishing Amelee Rives's *The Quick and the Dead* (1888) and other radical works. In 1934 Lippincott published Zora Neale Hurston's first novel, *Jonah's Gourd Vine* and published all of her later works except *Moses, Man of the Mountain.*
50. Meant as a southern counterpoint to *Uncle Tom's Cabin,* the book was widely read and popular, though not on a scale with Stowe's seminal work.

51. William Parker, "The Freedman's Story," *The Atlantic Monthly,* February/March 1866, 152.
52. Here I have limited my study to publications in book form. For a discussion of the development of antislavery literature in periodicals and magazines, see Sanchez-Eppler, *Touching Liberty,* 22–24. The sample I focus on here includes the works of those novelists who published in the United States between 1845 and 1870—the period known as "the golden age of slave narratives."

Chapter 3

1. Cooke's first story was published in *Graham's Magazine* (1845); her first verses appeared in the *New York Tribune* under the editorship of Charles A. Dana, to whom she dedicated her book of poems in 1861 (Harriet Prescott Spofford, "Rose Terry Cooke," *Our Famous Women* (Hartford: A. D. Worthington and Co., 1884), 190–91; letter to James T. Fields, 21 July 1860, Huntington Library. "The Mormon's Wife," was the story, however, that established her readership; it was published in *Putnam's* V(July 1855): 641–49.
2. Kenneth Price and Susan Belasco Smith, eds., *Periodical Literature in Nineteenth-Century America* (Charlottesville: U of Virginia P, 1995), 5. Among those that published both Cooke and works by slaves and about slavery were *The Atlantic Monthly, The Christian Examiner,* and *Putnam's Monthly Magazine* (Charles T. Davis and Henry Louis Gates, Jr., *The Slave's Narrative* (New York: Oxford, 1985).
3. Richard Brodhead's *Culture of Letters* (Chicago: U of Illinois P, 1986); William Charvat's *Literary Publishing in America, 1790–1850* (Amherst: U of Mass P, 1959; rpt. 1993.); David Hall's *Cultures of Print* (Amherst: U of Massachusetts P, 1996); Susan Coultrap-McQuinn's *Doing Literary Business: American Women Writers in the Nineteenth Century* (Chapel Hill: U of North Carolina P, 1990); Kenneth Price and Susan Belasco Smith's *Periodical Literature in Nineteenth-Century America;* Michael Winship's *American Literary Publishing in the Mid-Nineteenth Century: The Business of Ticknor and Fields* (Cambridge, Cambridge UP, 1995); and Sandra Zagarell's "Crosscurrents: Registers of Nordicism, Community, and Culture in Jewett's *Country of Pointed Firs,*" (*The Yale Journal of Criticism* 10 [1997]: 355–70) have guided me in my thinking. Zagarell's "Crosscurrents" has been especially helpful in its suggestion that we consider the various "registers" of discourse as simultaneous and constitutive, rather than mutually exclusive.
4. The only other source published by a contemporary—*A Little Book of Friends* (1916)—was also written by Spofford (Little, Brown, 1916), 143–56.
5. *Our Famous Women.* "By the following twenty eminent authors: Elizabeth Stuart Phelps, Harriet Beecher Stowe, Rose Terry Cooke . . . Harriet Prescott Spofford, Marion Harland . . . Louise Chandler Moulton, Mrs. A. D. T. Whitney, Lucy Larcom, Julia Ward Howe, Susan Coolidge [pseud.],

Kate Sanborn, Elizabeth Cady Stanton [etc.]." (Hartford, CT: A. D. Worthington & Co.; Chicago, IL, A.G. Nettleton & Co., 1884,) 190. The entry on Cooke was written by Spofford.

6. After the 1861 publication of *Poems,* Ticknor and Fields published her short fiction only. So, despite the fact that the poetry exhibits some of the same rhetorical strategies I am discussing here—a fact treated very briefly by Cheryl Walker in a "profile" of Cooke for *Legacy* in 1992 (vol. 9, 2: 143–50)—it does not represent the kind of market phenomenon that the short fiction does. Thus, I have elected not to consider her poetry here.
7. Spofford reports five episodes of impersonation. Elizabeth Ammons also discusses these events in her introduction to Rose Terry Cooke, *How Celia Changed Her Mind and Selected Stories,* ed. Elizabeth Ammons (New Brunswick: Rutgers UP, 1986).
8. Kenneth Price and Susan Belasco Smith, eds., *Periodical Literature in Nineteenth-Century America,* 3, emphasis added.
9. By 1860, the masthead read, "A Magazine of Literature, Science, Art, and Politics." In that year, it also included Asa Gray's review of Darwin's *Origin of the Species.*
10. For a study of Ticknor and Fields's innovations in the publishing business, see Winship, *American Literary Publishing in the Mid-Nineteenth Century: The Business of Ticknor and Fields.*
11. Winship, *American Literary Publishing in the Mid-Nineteenth Century: The Business of Ticknor and Fields.*
12. Until recently, Cooke's works have not been republished and thus have not followed other noted trends used to promote the canonized New England writers. "In later years," Winship observes, "these texts were republished in new forms—in pocket editions, in school textbooks, in a set or volume of collected works—that both reinforced and altered public understanding and the evaluation of their worth." (*American Literary Publishing in the Mid-Nineteenth Century: The Business of Ticknor and Fields,* 191). Cooke's works have not been popularized in this fashion, which may have something to do with her loss of a reading public. After her death, her work was not reprinted until the 1960s and then, most recently, in the collection edited by Elizabeth Ammons called *How Celia Changed Her Mind and Other Stories.*
13. *Poems* (1861), *Happy Dodd* (1878), *Somebody's Neighbors* (1881), *The Sphinx's Children and Other Stories* (1886), *Steadfast* (1889), and *Huckleberries Gathered from New England Hills* (1891) were published by Ticknor and Fields or their ensigns. In addition, *The Atlantic Monthly*—also published by Ticknor and Fields—was a frequent source for new Cooke material. *The Deacon's Week* (1884), *Rootbound and Other Sketches* (1885), and *The Old Garden* (1888) were published elsewhere. *Little Foxes* (1904) was published posthumously in Philadelphia by H. Altemus.
14. For a discussion of the "gentleman publishers," among them, Ticknor and Fields, see Coultrap-McQuinn, *Doing Literary Business.*

15. Rose Terry Cooke to Ticknor and Fields, 16 March 1861, courtesy of the Huntington Library.
16. Perhaps one of the best examples of Ticknor and Fields, in their later incarnation of Houghton Mifflin, overriding an author's wishes is the publication history of Charles Chesnutt's *The Conjure Woman and Other Tales* (Boston: Houghton Mifflin, 1899). As Richard Brodhead details in his "Introduction" to Charles W. Chesnutt, *The Conjure Woman and Other Conjure Tales* (Durham: Duke UP, 1993), "What we have in *The Conjure Woman* is a work partly proposed by an author but also in significant part imagined by a publisher, then written by the author to the publisher's specifications. The publisher then chose the volume's contents from the batch of tales Chesnutt submitted, so that this book, apparently complete in itself, in fact embodies a selection, one version of Chesnutt's work carved from a much larger, and much more diverse, body of writing."
17. Rose Terry Cooke to Ticknor and Fields, 16 March 1861, courtesy of the Huntington Library.
18. Ellery Sedgwick, *The Atlantic Monthly, 1857–1909: Yankee Humanism at High Tide* (Amherst: U of Massachusetts P, 1994), 71.
19. Sedgwick, *The Atlantic Monthly, 1857–1909,* 70.
20. Sedgwick, *The Atlantic Monthly, 1857–1909,* 69.
21. Sedgwick, *The Atlantic Monthly, 1857–1909,* 83.
22. Subscriber Book, Boston Public Library.
23. Until that time, Frances had assisted his father with typesetting and other duties associated with publishing the well-known abolitionist newspaper.
24. For a discussion of the market for antislavery stories see Karen Sanchez-Eppler's *Touching Liberty: Abolition, Feminism, and the Politics of the Body* (Berkeley: U of California P, 1993), 23–26; 152–53.
25. Rose Terry Cooke, "Sally Parson's Duty," *The Atlantic Monthly* 1(Nov 1857):24–33; "The Ring Fetter" *The Atlantic Monthly* 4 (August 1859)154–70; rpt. in *How Celia Changed Her Mind and Selected Stories,* ed. Elizabeth Ammons (New Brunswick: Rutgers UP, 1986), 37. Unless otherwise noted, all page references to Cooke's stories will be to this edition.
26. Cooke, "Sally Parson's Duty," 25.
27. Cooke, "Sally Parson's Duty," 29.
28. Cooke, "Sally Parson's Duty," 26–27.
29. Cooke, "Sally Parson's Duty," 24.
30. Cooke, "Sally Parson's Duty," 33.
31. For further discussion of popular culture's representation of blacks in the antebellum period, see Eric Lott, *Love and Theft: Black Minstrelsy and the American Working Class* (New York: Oxford UP, 1993); David Roediger, *The Wages of Whiteness: Race and the Making of the American Working Class* (London: Verso, 1991); Alexander Saxton, *The Rise and Fall of the White Republic: Class Politics and Mass Culture in Nineteenth-Century America* (London: Verso, 1990). The phrase quoted in the text is taken from Jean

Baker, *Affairs of Party: The Political Culture of Northern Democrats in the Mid-Nineteenth Century* (Ithaca: Cornell UP, 1983), 225.

32. Cooke, "Sally Parson's Duty," 28.
33. Cooke, "Sally Parson's Duty," 28.
34. Cooke, "Sally Parson's Duty," 28.
35. Elizabeth B. Clark, "'The Sacred Rights of the Weak': Pain, Sympathy, and the Culture of Individual Rights in Antebellum America," *The Journal of American History* (September 1995): 463–93, 487.
36. Cooke, "The Ring Fetter," 36.
37. Cooke, "The Ring Fetter," 38.
38. Cooke, "The Ring Fetter," 42.
39. Cooke, "The Ring Fetter," 42.
40. Cooke, "The Ring Fetter," 42.
41. Cooke, "The Ring Fetter," 40–43.
42. Cooke, "The Ring Fetter," 46.
43. Cooke, "The Ring Fetter," 49.
44. Cooke, "The Ring Fetter," 49.
45. Cooke, "The Ring Fetter," 49.
46. Cooke, "The Ring Fetter," 53.
47. Cooke, "The Ring Fetter." 53
48. Cooke, "The Ring Fetter," 42.
49. For a full discussion of the class affiliations of sentimentalism, see Amy Schrager Lang, "Class and the Strategies of Sympathy" in *The Culture of Sentiment,* ed. Shirley Samuels (New York: Oxford UP, 1992).
50. Hazel V. Carby, *Reconstructing Womanhood* (New York: Oxford UP, 1987), 49.
51. Cooke to Howells, 26 November 1880, bMS Am 1784 (106); quoted by permission of the Houghton Library, Harvard University.
52. Despite critical speculation to this end, all reports of the marriage portray it as a happy one.
53. Cooke, "Mrs. Flint's Married Experience," rpt. in *How Celia Changed Her Mind and Selected Stories,* ed. Elizabeth Ammons (New Brunswick: Rutgers UP, 1986), 112
54. Cooke, "Mrs. Flint's Married Experience," 99.
55. Cooke, "Mrs. Flint's Married Experience," 123.
56. Jean Edward Smith, *Grant* (New York: Simon and Schuster, 2001).
57. Cooke, "Mrs. Flint's Married Experience," 126.
58. Cooke, "Mrs. Flint's Married Experience," 96.
59. Cooke, "Mrs. Flint's Married Experience," 96.
60. Cooke, "Mrs. Flint's Married Experience," 122.
61. According to Ammons, in her introduction to *How Celia Changed Her Mind and Selected Stories,* this story did not appear in a periodical (xxxix).
62. Cooke, "How Celia Changed Her Mind," rpt. In Ammons, *How Celia Changed Her Mind and Selected Stories,* 149–150.
63. Michael Grossberg, *Governing the Hearth: Law and the Family in Nineteenth-Century America* (Chapel Hill: U of North Carolina P, 1985), 268.

64. Cooke, "How Celia Changed Her Mind," 145.
65. Cooke, "How Celia Changed Her Mind," 145.
66. Rose Terry Cooke, "A Hard Lesson," *The Continent* 5 (June 1884): 682–88, 683.
67. Cooke, "A Hard Lesson," 684, emphasis mine.
68. Quoted in Patricia Hill, "Painting Race" in *Eastman Johnson, Painting America,* ed. Teresa A. Carbone and Patricia Hills, with contributions by Jane Weiss, Sarah Burns, and Anne C. Rose (New York: Brooklyn Museum of Art in association with Rizzoli International Publications, 1999), 162.
69. Spofford recounts the story in which Cooke donates an opal ring—the only thing of value she had on her person—one day when Henry Ward Beecher was raising money to free a slave child. According to her, the occasion has been memorialized in "Freedom Ring," a painting by Eastman Johnson (202–3). For additional information, see Patricia Hill, "Painting Race," in *Eastman Johnson, Painting America.*
70. "Our Slave," *The Independent* XL (Nov 8, 1888) 1450–51.
71. Elizabeth Clark, in "'The Sacred Rights of the Weak' Pain, Sympathy, and the Culture of Individual Rights in Antebellum America," discusses the link between the suffering slave body and the rise of individual rights, especially within the context of marriage.
72. Cooke, "How Celia Changed Her Mind," 151.
73. Rose Terry Cooke, "Miss Lucinda," *The Atlantic Monthly,* 8 August 1861.
74. Here Cooke further departs from larger tendencies in local color literature; Lucinda's suitor is not just an outsider, he is a foreigner. Thus Cooke does not exhibit the "edginess" about foreigners that other local colorists do (Zagarell, "Exclusion of Difference").
75. Cooke, "Miss Lucinda," 151.
76. Cooke, "Sally Parson's Duty," 28.
77. Rose Terry Cooke, "Miss Lucinda," *The Atlantic Monthly,* 8 Aug 1861.
78. Rose Terry Cooke to James Field, 2 Oct 1864, quoted by permission of the Huntington Library.
79. Howells, William Dean. "The Man of Literature as a Man of Business," *Literature and Life* (New York: Harper's, 1902).
80. For a discussion of Hawthorne's relative gain in adopting the novel form see William Charvat, *Literary Publishing in America, 1790–1850* (Amherst: U of Massachusetts P, 1959); Richard Brodhead, *The School of Hawthorne* (New York: Oxford, 1993); Teresa Goddu, *Gothic America: Narrative, History, and Nation* (New York: Columbia UP, 1997), 94–116.
81. Winship, *American Literary Publishing in the Mid-Nineteenth Century: The Business of Ticknor and Fields,* 191.
82. Quoted in Cheryl Walker, "Rose Terry Cooke," *Legacy,* 9 (1992): 146.
83. James Russell Lowell cut his editorial teeth at the *Anti- Slavery Standard* in 1848, his first job in publishing. Other editors, such as William Dean Howells, also had connections to abolition.

84. Once again, I am borrowing the term "registers" from Sandra Zagarell, "Crosscurrents: Registers of Noricism, Community, and Culture in Jewett's *Country of Pointed Firs.*"
85. Russ Castronovo's "Incidents in the Life of a White Woman: Economics of Race and Gender in the Antebellum Nation" (*American Literary History* 10 (Summer 1998): 2:239–65) is among the most recent contributions to this task.

Chapter 4

1. William Dean Howells, quoted in Alan Trachtenberg, *The Incorporation of America: Culture and Society in the Gilded Age* (New York: Hill and Wang, 1982), 185.
2. "Dialect in Literature," *Harper's,* 8 June 1895; rpt. vol. 21 of *The Collected Works,* 220.
3. Willa Cather, "William Dean Howells," *Nebraska State Journal,* 14 July 1895, quoted in *Cather: Stories, Poems and Other Writings,* ed. Sharon O'Brien (New York: Library of America, 1992), 892.
4. For a full discussion of the Civil War memoir, its popularity, and marketability, see David Blight, *Race and Reunion: The Civil War in American Memory* (Cambridge: Harvard UP, 2001), 140–211.
5. David Blight, *Race and Reunion,* 175.
6. Rodney D. Olsen, in *Dancing in Chains: The Youth of William Dean Howells* (New York: New York UP, 1991) details Howells' relationship to the abolitionist movement.
7. Olsen, *Dancing in Chains,* 175.
8. The Howells family commitment to abolition forced the family to relocate several times. See Crowley's *The Black Heart's Truth* (Chapel Hill: U of North Carolina P, 1985) and Olsen's *Dancing in Chains* for a more detailed discussion of the impact of his father's Free Soiler sentiments and the subsequent dislocations they caused on the young Howells.
9. The quotation from the *New York Times* appeared in Nina Silber (*The Romance of Reunion: Northerners and the South, 1865–1900* (Chapel Hill: U of North Carolina P, 1993), 62.
10. This photograph is dated 1882. All of the photographs discussed here are part of the William Dean Howells collection at Houghton Library, Harvard University (pMS Am 1784.3 [36]).
11. bMS Am 1784.3 (3), Leather-bound, red silk-lined daily pocket diary "for the year 1860: for the purpose of registering events of past, present, and future occurrence." Published by Kiggins and Kellogg, a New York firm of publishers, booksellers, stationers & blank book manufacturers. It is inscribed, "W. D. Howells from A. L. H."—clearly a gift from his sister.
12. Weather records were popular among farmers as a way to create their own almanacs and also as a way to keep track of time through experience. In Howells's case, he seemed to be drawing on this practice but not enjoying

it as there are only a few entries of this sort. My thanks to Ellen Gruber Garvey for drawing out this detail during the discussion period of the MLA session where this paper was first presented in 1998.

13. Howells, entry dated 14 September 1860.
14. Howells, entries, dated 3 and 8 March 1860.
15. Ironically, Howells's signature ended up becoming a "trademark"; it often appeared on the cover of his books in gilt letters.
16. This entry is undated.
17. William Charvat, "Longfellow's Income from his Writings, 1842–1852," *The Profession of Authorship in America 1800–1870* (Columbus: Ohio State UP, 1968).
18. BMS Am 1784.3 (12).
19. Anesko, *Letters, Fictions, Lives: Henry James and William Dean Howells* (NY: Oxford UP, 1997), 32. Of course, just because James criticized Howells, does not mean he did not also regret not being more financially successful himself. For instance, in response to Howells's praise of James's reputation, James replied, "My fame indeed seems to do well everywhere . . . it's only my fortune that leaves to be desired." James to Howells, quoted in Anesko, *Letters, Fictions, Lives,* 134.
20. According to John J. McCusker's "How Much is That in Real Money? A Historical Price Index for Use as a Deflator of Money Value in the Economy of the United States" (Proceedings of the American Antiquarian Society 101, pt. 2 1992, 297–373), we should use an 18:1 ratio to estimate Howells's financial situation in today's values. His $60,000 would be approximately $1,080,000 by today's standards. The figure he provided for 1892 ($68,409.81) translates to roughly $1,231,375. The $10,000 in stereotype plates, then, would calculate to approximately $180,000. By this same measure, Howells's annual income from old copy rights and rental property comes to about $60,000.
21. (folder 2).
22. (bMS Am 1784.3 [9] [Contracts for works no longer in copyright]- folder 1.) (folder 2). As early as his contract for *Venetian Life and Italian Journeys,* Howells made certain of the right to purchase stereotype plates at cost. There, as in other contracts, he agreed to maintain publication rights with Houghton as long as he could own the plates. By 1885, Howells was consistently supplying the plates for the publisher's use.
23. Howells, together with his good friend Mark Twain and others, anticipated that stereotype plates would take on added value as the fight to extend copyright continued to make strides. By 1909, Twain joined forces with authors and publishers and thereby succeeded in expanding the terms of copyright from 28 years with renewal for 14 years to 28 years with a 28-year renewal. Coincidentally, this action, brought about by a visit to Congress, also marked the debut of Twain's trademark white suit.

    Owning the stereotype plates meant controlling how many editions were printed. Up through 1820, authors lost control of their works when they did not own the plates because publishers could sell copies of the plates to other printers, who then made and sold additional copies of the printed book without paying the author a share. In the period after Washington Irving and James Fenimore Cooper, authors began to purchase the plates with the profits of the first printing of their works, if they could afford to do so. By owning the plates, authors sold the right to print the book as well as negotiated for a profit in the sales themselves.

24. But these figures don't record the difficulty that Howells and his family underwent in order to build his career. The choice to move from Boston to New York and take up the position of editor at *Harper's* was laden with disappointment. Rather than sell it, the Howells let their house in Cambridge. According to the Howells, when they bought that house, they had planned to live in it for the rest of their lives; they ended up staying for only six years. Retaining the property as a rental speaks to their reluctance to give up the lifestyle the house signified for them and the value they placed on it. Howells's putting the house at the top of his list of assets implies its special status.
25. bMS AM 1784.3 (12).
26. Howells did publish one poem on a racial subject, "A Pilot's Story," published in *The Atlantic Monthly* vol. 6, no. 6 (September 1860): 323–25. The poem reounts the tagic tale of an octoroon—treated as a wife but sold as a slave. My thanks to Werner Sollers for reminding me of this publication.
27. And inversely, when he did not care to write on a subject—as was the case when *Harper's* asked him to write a memoir of the recently deceased Henry James—he priced the essay beyond the market to avoid writing it rather than simply refusing the assignment. Kenneth S. Lynn, *William Dean Howells, An American Life* (NY: Harcourt, Brace, Jovanovich, 1970), 322–30.
28. bMS Am 1784 (353).
29. Reports about how *A Modern Instance* was doing, for example, were included as a regular topic for consideration during the negotiation process for the publication of *Silas Lapham* in a letter that passed between Howells and his publisher/agent, James R. Osgood.
30. Nearly $50,000 in today's terms. The Easy Chair earnings would have brought this figure up over $70,000.
31. Individual tax payments were $403.51, $371.23, and $613.34 respectively.
32. No records of mortgage payments appear in these files which include checkbooks and account payments from three banks. I did find monthly maintenance payments recorded in the checkbooks. But these sums amount to less than the amounts listed as "income" for the New York apartments.
33. Howells was also offered James Russell Lowell's old job at Harvard—one occupied by Longfellow before him. Howells, for all the same reasons as with the Johns Hopkins appointment, turned down the job.
34. bMS Am 1784(301), letter 29.
35. William Dean Howells, *Hazard of New Fortunes* (New York: Harper & Bros., 1890), 7.
36. Not knowing his first name is especially remarkable since, during the course of the novel, he courts and eventually marries another character.

Thus, despite the fact that readers encounter him outside of the business world, his identity remains businesslike.

37. Howells will return to this fictional couple two more times in his career in *An Open-Eyed Conspiracy* (1897) and its sequel, *Their Silver Wedding Journey* (1899).
38. Howells uses this same device to link *A Modern Instance* to *The Rise of Silas Lapham;* Bartley Hubbard, a protagonist in *A Modern Instance,* makes a cameo appearance as a reporter in the later novel.
39. According to John W. Crowley, Howells's use of March as a narrative voice was a form of ventriloquism. Speaking from behind what Howells called "the mask of fiction" allowed him to explore complex social issues without being tied to a particular position. Crowley, "The Unsmiling Aspects of Life: A Hazard of New Fortunes," in *Biographies of Books,* ed. Thomas Quirk, (Columbia: U Missouri P, 1996), 78–110.
40. Howells, *Hazard of New Fortunes,* 89. See also "American Literary Centers," in *Literature and Life* (NY: Harper's, 1902).
41. Howells, *Hazard of New Fortunes,* 182.
42. Here Howells aligns his views with modern-day labor historians such as David Roedigger's *The Wages of Whiteness: Race and the Making of the American Working Class* (London: Verso, 1991). Roedigger, following in the steps of Herb Guttman, would applaud Howells's link of abolition to the wage labor movement through the character of Lindau.
43. Howells, *Hazard of New Fortunes,* 108.
44. Cf. David Sheilds's study of eighteenth century authorship, *Civil Tongues & Polite Letters in British America* (Chapel Hill: U of North Carolina P [for the Institute of Early American History and Culture, Williamsburg VA], 1997).
45. Howells, *Hazard of New Fortunes,* 108.
46. Howells, *Hazard of New Fortunes,* 183.
47. Howells mirrors his personal relationship to socialism by endorsing these activities in the novel. Cf. John Crowely on Howells's "theoretical" socialism versus his "practical" capitalism ("The Unsmiling Aspects"). It seems that though he endorsed the values of socialism represented according to his mentor Tolstoy, he did not want to give up the luxuries that his life's work had yielded.
48. Byron is an important example of this phenomenon. He appeared, shirt unbuttoned, the very image of the romantic poet. Other celebrated images of authorship are Walt Whitman as one of the "roughs" and Mark Twain in his trademark white suit.
49. In "Eaten Alive: Slavery and Celebrity in Antebellum America," Michael Newbury argues that slavery and celebrity share the same model of labor. His analysis turns on the realization that both the slave and the celebrity are embodied forms of property.
50. Kenneth Lynn, in *William Dean Howells: An American Life,* crops this photograph and turns it into a head shot of Howells.
51. In *The Road to Realism* (Syracuse: Syracuse UP, 1956), Edwin Cady documents Howells's deliberate turn away from journalism and politics as significant of his aspiration to be a man of letters.

52. Howells, "American Literary Centers," 189.
53. Howells, "American Literary Centers," 184.
54. These novels use travel as a means to suggest intimacy by inviting the reader to "share" these memories by creating them together through the process of the story. Howells is a master host, sharing his privileges with his readers and teaching them how to attain their own comfort. And that's part of what making people comfortable is all about.
55. Michael Davitt Bell, *The Problem of American Realism* (Chicago: U of Chicago P, 1993), following Alfred Habegger *Gender, Fantasy, and Realism in American Literature* (New York: Columbia UP, 1982), treats Howells's choice as part of Howells' larger project to reconcile his identity as an artist with the cultural pressure to be a man and therefore be in business. At mid-century, when Howells first dreamed of becoming a writer, Boston was the center for the literary man who made a living by the pen such as Longfellow. Thus Howells's ambition to be a writer seemed most capable of being fulfilled in Boston.
56. See Michael Davitt Bell, *The Problem of American Realism,* (Chicago: U of Chicago P, 1993).
57. Howells, "American Literary Centers," 179.
58. As I mentioned earlier, in another envelope marked "WDH w/o his mustache" there is a statement written in the hand of Mildred Howells indicating that permission to reproduce this photograph will not be granted during the lifetime of the undersigned, literary heirs that include his son and daughter, John Mead Howells and Mildred Howells.
59. Nathaniel Hawthorne observed that the face of American manhood had been changed by a European fashion: the mustache. Marcus Cunliffe, *The Nation Takes Shape.* (Chicago: U of Chicago P, 1989), 182.

Chapter 5

1. Edith Wharton, *A Backward Glance* (New York: Scribner, 1933; rpt., 1963), 146.
2. Wharton reports this observation in *A Backward Glance,* 147.
3. Scholarship on Wharton's place in realism has been copious; the works of Amy Kaplan and Wei-Chee Dimock have been especially helpful to me.
4. Many have written on this topic and I will be addressing their work throughout the course of this chapter. However, essays by Elizabeth Ammons, Irene Goldman-Price, Hildegarde Hoeller, and Jennie Kassanoff are at the center of the issues I'd like to discuss here.
5. Wharton, *A Backward Glance,* 206.
6. Shari Benstock, *No Gifts From Chance: A Biography of Edith Wharton* (New York: Charles Scribner's Sons, 199), 142.
7. Benstock, *No Gifts From Chance,* 142.
8. David Roediger uncovers the racist structures of early thinking about class in the United States in *The Wages of Whiteness: Race and the Making of the American Working Class* (London: Verso, 1991).

9. For an ethnographic and anthropological reading of Wharton's work, see Nancy Bentley's "'Hunting for the Real': Wharton and the Science of Manners" in *The Cambridge Companion to Edith Wharton,* ed. Millicent Bell (New York: Cambridge UP, 1995).
10. Wharton, "Permanent Values in Fiction" in *The Uncollected Critical Writings,* ed. Frederick Wegener (Princeton: Princeton UP, 1996), 175. In *A Backward Glance,* Wharton tells readers that her mother lumped Stowe in with a broad list of novelists, calling her "so common and so successful," 65.
11. Wharton, *A Backward Glance,* 94.
12. *Edith Wharton's Library—A Catalogue,* compiled by George Ramsden with a foreword by Hermonie Lee (Settington, England: Stone Trough Books, 1999).
13. Wharton, "Permanent Values," 177, 176.
14. Wharton, "Permanent Values," 176.
15. The reigning theory, on both sides of the color line, was always that the blacker the body, the lower the class. The idea is that the more visible racial traits are, the more pronounced are the attributes of social class. Recall, for instance, Lawrence Selden's observation that Lily's hand is "polished as a bit of old ivory" (6), thus associating skin color with the class that can afford ivory or even antique ivory at that. See Judith R. Berzon's *Neither Black nor White* (New York: New York UP, 1978); James Kinney's *Amalgamation! Race, Sex, and the Rhetoric of the 19th Century American Novel* (Westport, CT: Greenood, 1985); John Mencke's *Mulattos and Race Mixture* (UMI Research P, 1979); as well as Werner Sollers's "'Never Was Born': The Mulatto, An American Tragedy?" (*Massachusetts Review* 27 (1986 Summer): 293–316 for further discussion of the history of the tragic mulatto/a as a literary figure.
16. In *Edith Wharton's Brave New Politics* (Madison: U of Wisconsin P, 1994), Dale Bauer links Wharton's later work with political and social theories of that period, including eugenics, capitalism, and free love.
17. Wharton, *House of Mirth,* 140.
18. Wharton, *House of Mirth,* 141.
19. Wharton, *House of Mirth,* 4.
20. Wharton, *House of Mirth,* 4.
21. Wharton, *House of Mirth,* 278.
22. Wharton, *House of Mirth,* 179.
23. Wharton, *House of Mirth,* 7.
24. Wharton, *House of Mirth,* 136.
25. Wharton, *House of Mirth,* 97.
26. Wharton, *House of Mirth,* 6.
27. Wharton, *House of Mirth,* 4.
28. According to Judith Fryer (*Felicitous Space: The Imaginative Structures of Edith Wharton and Willa Cather* [Chapel Hill: U of North Carolina P, 1986]), Wharton draws upon her knowledge of fine arts (particularly Italian Renaissance painting), upon literary precedents (George Eliot's *Daniel Deroda,* for example, in which Gwendolyn Harleth poses in a tableau vivant as

Saint Cecilia), upon contemporary bestsellers (like Constance Cary Harrison's *The Anglomaniacs* [1890], in which another Lily . . . attends a ball where the table is set out to represent a Veronese painting and she herself is dressed as a Venetian princess, and upon the popularity of tableaux vivants as entertainment in late-nineteenth-century America (29).

29. Wharton, *House of Mirth,* 166.
30. Wharton, *House of Mirth,* 135.
31. Edith Wharton, *Summer* (New York: Scribner's, 1916; rpt. Library of America, 1990), 275; *Age of Innocence* (New York: Appelton, 1920; rpt. Library of America, 1985), 1184.
32. Lewis describes the shock and dismay of contemporary readers to Lily Bart's demise. One reader, he reported, "said that when she read the final installment, she was so overcome that she telegraphed a friend, 'Lily Bart is dead'" (R. W. B. Lewis, *Edith Wharton: A Biography* [New York: Fromm International, 1985], 152). When I teach the novel, students always respond with sorrow and disappointment that Lily Bart must die.
33. Wharton, *House of Mirth,* 55.
34. Wharton, *House of Mirth,* 45.
35. Wharton, *House of Mirth,* 87.
36. See Benstock, "'The word which made all clear': The Silent Close of *The House of Mirth,*" *Famous Last Words: Changes in Gender and Narrative Closure* (Charlottesville: U of Virginia P, 1993), 241–43.
37. Wharton, *A Backward Glance,* 206, my emphasis.
38. This term, "social geography" is taken from Ruth Frankenberg, *White Women, Race Matters: The Social Construction of Whiteness* (Minneapolis: U of Minnesota P, 1993). According to Frankenberg, "social geography suggests that the physical landscape is peopled and that it is constituted and perceived by means of social rather than natural processes" (43–44). The term is especially useful when speaking of Wharton's "old New York" since the people that make up this community define the place.
39. Wharton, *A Backward Glance,* 207.
40. Wharton, *A Backward Glance,* 73.
41. This interpretation departs from the standard critical reading of the relationship between Wharton's life and the effect her experiences had on her work. For the most recent analysis of Lucretia Jones's remark, see Benstock (*No Gifts From Chance,* 35), who, taking her cue from Wharton herself, reads this experience as a purely negative one: "With this acerbic comment ringing in her ears, Edith turned from fiction to poetry" (35).
42. Lewis, *Edith Wharton: A Biography,* 145.
43. Frankenburg, *White Women, Race Matters,* 13.
44. Lewis, *Edith Wharton: A Biography,* 144.
45. Trans., R. W.B. Lewis, *The Letters of Edith Wharton* ed. R. W. B. Lewis (New York: Collier, 1988), 159.
46. Henry Louis Gates, Jr., *Figures in Black* (New York: Oxford, 1987), xvii.
47. As I will discuss later in this essay, Wharton underwrites this conception of class with Carry Fisher in *The House of Mirth.*

48. Shari Benstock, "A Critical History of *The House of Mirth,*" in Edith Wharton, *The House of Mirth,* ed. Shari Benstock (Boston: Bedford Books, 1994), 311.
49. Wharton, *House of Mirth,* 10.
50. Wharton, *A Backward Glance,* 207.
51. Wharton's reprehensibly racist attitudes and actions are discussed in Benstock's *No Gifts from Chance.*
52. See n16.
53. Wharton, *A Backward Glance,* 206.
54. Wharton, *House of Mirth,* 216.
55. Several important essays—among them Irene Goldman-Price's "The Perfect Jew and *The House of Mirth:* A Study in Point of View," *Modern Language Studies* 23: 2 (1993): 25–36; Hildegarde Hoeller's "'The Impossible Rosedale': 'Race' and the Reading of Edith Wharton's *House of Mirth,*" *Studies in American Jewish Literature* 13 (1994): 14–20; and Jennie Kassanoff's "Extinction, Taxidermy, Tableau Vivants: Staging Race and Class in *The House of Mirth,*" *PMLA* 115: 1 (January 2000): 60–74—have recently explored the pretense of race as a model for identity in Edith Wharton's *House of Mirth.* I am not here to add my voice to their intriguing readings, but rather to redirect our attention to race's function as a narrative device.
56. See Ammons, Bell, and Bently in *The Cambridge Companion to Edith Wharton,* ed. Millicent Bell.
57. Here I am taking issue with Kassanoff's decision to limit the meaning of race in *The House of Mirth.* As I discuss in what follows, Wharton seems to capitalize on the way that race vibrates across class lines tragically. Thus "race" is as much a narrative strategy as any other "trope."
58. See Kassanoff.
59. Wharton, *House of Mirth,* 19.
60. Wharton, *House of Mirth,* 19.
61. Wharton, *A Backward Glance,* 206.
62. *Letters,* 98.
63. *Letters,* 98.
64. *Letters,* 47.
65. *Letters,* 48.
66. *Letters,* 48.
67. Wharton, *A Backward Glance,* 200.
68. *Letters,* 94.
69. Wharton, *House of Mirth,* 32.
70. Gates, *Figures In Black,* 173.

Epilogue

1. The phrase comes from Thomas Laqueur, "Bodies, Details, and the Humanitarian Narrative" (*The New Cultural History,* ed. Lynn Hunt [Berkeley: U of California P, 1989] 176–205).

2. David Blight, *Race and Reunion: The Civil War in American Memory* (Cambridge: Harvard UP, 2001).
3. Philip Fisher, in *Hard Facts: Setting and Form in the American Novel* (New York: Oxford, 1987), sees the impact of industrialization and the rise of the city as both the stimulus for and the focal point of post-Reconstruction fiction.
4. According to the Publishers Weekly list (http://www.caderbooks.com/best00.html), the top ten sellers of 1905 were:
    1. *The Marriage of William Ashe,* Mary Augusta Ward
    2. *Sandy,* Alice Hegan Rice
    3. *The Garden of Allah,* Robert Hichens
    4. *The Clansman,* Thomas Dixon Jr.
    5. *Nedra,* George Barr McCutcheon
    6. *The Gambler,* Katherine Cecil Thurston
    7. *The Masquerader,* anonymous (Katherine Cecil Thurston)
    8. *The House of Mirth,* Edith Wharton
    9. *The Princess Passes,* C. N. and A. M. Williamson
    10. *Rose o' the River,* Kate Douglas Wiggin
5. British director Terence Davies remade *The House of Mirth* (2000) starring Eric Stolz and Gillian Anderson. Despite his ingenious casting, however, the film did not do well with audiences.
6. Ida B. Wells, *Southern Horrors: Lynch Law in all its Phases* (1892), rpt. Boston: Bedford Books, 1997.
7. His first bestseller was *The Foxes of Yarrow* (1946) followed by *The Vixens* (1947), *Floodtide* (1950), *A Woman Called Fancy* (1951), *The Saracen Blade* (1952), and *Benton's Row* (1954). My thanks to Richard Newman for bringing Yerby to my attention.
8. The *Publisher's Weekly* list is the longest-running bestseller list. I have used it as a source for this reason as well as the fact that this is the list developed with an eye to the publishing business rather than to the readership as with later lists such as the *New York Times* list, established in 1942.
9. In addition to the *House of Mirth* in 1905, Wharton had *The Age of Innocence* (for which she won a Pulizter) and *Twilight Sleep* in 1921 and 1927 respectively on the bestseller list. Willa Cather's *Shadows on the Rock* was a bestseller in 1931 and like Cather, William Faulkner also had one book on the bestseller list: *The Reivers* (1962). Hemingway was more successful marketwise; he had four books make the bestseller list: *For Whom the Bell Tolls* (1940), *Across the River and Into the Trees* (1950), *The Old Man and the Sea* (1952) and *Islands in the Stream* (1970). Sinclair Lewis's *Main Street,* his first of ten bestsellers, shared space with Wharton's *Age of Innocence* in 1921. John Steinbeck first entered the ranks of bestselling authors with his 1937 classic, *Of Mice and Men,* followed by *The Grapes of Wrath* (1939), *The Moon is Down* (1942), *The Wayward Blues* (1947), *East of Eden* (1952), *Sweet Thursday* (1954) and *The Winter of Our Discontent* (1961).

10. In the wake of *Uncle Tom's Cabin,* following Fisher's argument in *Hard Facts,* we lack the fundamental structures to re-imagine social justice for African Americans and thus this project becomes "unimaginable"(8).
11. See Martin Arnold, "Books by Blacks in Top Five Sellers," *New York Times,* 26 July 2001; C-3.

Index

Because *Truth Stranger than Fiction* does not have a bibliography, this index attempts to indicate references to secondary sources where the argument of a critic is discussed in some detail.

Numbers in **bold** refer to illustrations.